Elements of Literature®
Fifth Course

HOLT ASSESSMENT
Writing, Listening, and Speaking
Tests and Answer Key

- **Workshop Tests in Standardized Test Formats**
- **Evaluation Forms**
- **Scales and Rubrics**
- **Holistic Scoring Guides**
- **Analytical Scale: 7 Writing Traits**
- **Sample Papers**
- **Portfolio Assessment**

HOLT, RINEHART AND WINSTON
A Harcourt Education Company
Orlando • Austin • New York • San Diego • Toronto • London

Copyright © by Holt, Rinehart and Winston

All rights reserved. No part of this publication may be reproduced or transmitted in any form or by any means, electronic or mechanical, including photocopy, recording, or any information storage and retrieval system, without permission in writing from the publisher.

Teachers using ELEMENTS OF LITERATURE may photocopy blackline masters in complete pages in sufficient quantities for classroom use only and not for resale.

ELEMENTS OF LITERATURE, HOLT, and the "Owl Design" are trademarks licensed to Holt, Rinehart and Winston, registered in the United States of America and/or other jurisdictions.

Printed in the United States of America

If you have received these materials as examination copies free of charge, Holt, Rinehart and Winston retains title to the materials and they may not be resold. Resale of examination copies is strictly prohibited.

Possession of this publication in print format does not entitle users to convert this publication, or any portion of it, into electronic format.

ISBN 0-03-079007-7

5 6 179 07

Table of Contents

Overview of ELEMENTS OF LITERATURE Assessment Program vii

About This Book x

Writing Workshop Tests and Answer Key

Multiple-choice test for each Writing Workshop

for Collection 1
Writing Workshop: Editorial 3

for Collection 2
Writing Workshop: Short Story 7

for Collection 3
Writing Workshop: Reflective Essay 10

for Collection 4
Writing Workshop: Reporting Historical Research 13

for Collection 5
Writing Workshop: Analyzing a Novel 19

for Collection 6
Media Workshop: Analyzing and Using Media 22

Answer Sheet 1 25

Answer Sheet 2 26

Answer Key 27

Table of Contents *continued*

Workshop Scales and Rubrics

Analytical scales and scoring rubrics for
- Writing Workshops
- Listening and Speaking Workshops

for Collection 1
Writing: Editorial Scale and Rubric 33
Listening and Speaking:
  Presenting Speeches Scale 36

for Collection 2
Writing: Short Story Scale and Rubric 38

for Collection 3
Writing: Reflective Essay Scale and Rubric 41
Speaking: Presenting a Reflection Scale 44

for Collection 4
Writing: Reporting Historical Research Scale and Rubric 45
Speaking: Presenting Historical Research Scale 49

for Collection 5
Writing:
  Descriptive Essay Scale 50
  Analyzing Literature Scale 51
  Biographical Narrative Scale 52
  Analyzing a Novel Scale and Rubric 53
Speaking: Presenting a Literary Analysis Scale 56

for Collection 6
Writing:
  Autobiographical Narrative Scale 57
  Analyzing Nonfiction Scale 58
  Analyzing Media Scale 59
  Using Media Scale 60
Speaking: Reciting Literature Scale 61

Table of Contents *continued*

Scales and Sample Papers

Scales for assessing writing

Student sample papers with evaluations

Analytical Scale: 7 Writing Traits	**65**
Biographical or Autobiographical Narrative	
Holistic Scale	**72**
Sample Papers and Evaluations	**74**
Exposition	
Holistic Scale	**81**
Sample Papers and Evaluations	**83**
Response to Literature	
Holistic Scale	**90**
Sample Papers and Evaluations	**92**
Persuasion	
Holistic Scale	**99**
Sample Papers and Evaluations	**101**
Business Letter	
Holistic Scale	**108**
Sample Papers and Evaluations	**110**

Portfolio Assessment

An essay on portfolio management

Forms for evaluating writing, listening, and speaking

Portfolio Assessment in the Language Arts	**120**
How to Develop and Use Portfolios	**123**
Conferencing with Students	**132**
Questions and Answers	**136**
Portfolio Table of Contents	**142**
About This Portfolio	**143**
Home Review: What the Portfolio Shows	**145**
Home Response to the Portfolio	**146**
Writing Record	**147**
Spelling Log	**148**
Goal-Setting for Writing, Listening, and Speaking	**149**
Summary of Progress: Writing, Listening, and Speaking	**151**

Table of Contents *continued*

Writing Self-Inventory	153
Writing Process Self-Evaluation	154
Proofreading Strategies	155
Proofreading Checklist	156
Record of Proofreading Corrections	157
Multiple-Assignment Proofreading Record	158
Listening Self-Inventory	159
Speaking Self-Inventory	160
Skills Profile	161

FOR THE TEACHER

Overview of ELEMENTS OF LITERATURE Assessment Program

Two assessment booklets have been developed for ELEMENTS OF LITERATURE.

(1) Assessment of student mastery of selections and specific literary, reading, and vocabulary skills in the **Student Edition:**

- *Holt Assessment: Literature, Reading, and Vocabulary*

(2) Assessment of student mastery of workshops and specific writing, listening, and speaking skills in the **Student Edition:**

- *Holt Assessment: Writing, Listening, and Speaking*

Diagnostic Assessment

Holt Assessment: Literature, Reading, and Vocabulary contains two types of diagnostic tests:

- The Entry-Level Test is a diagnostic tool that helps you determine (1) how well students have mastered essential prerequisite skills needed for the year and (2) to what degree students understand the concepts that will be taught during the current year. This test uses multiple tasks to assess mastery of literary, reading, and vocabulary skills.

- The Collection Diagnostic Tests help you determine the extent of students' prior knowledge of literary, reading, and vocabulary skills taught in each collection. These tests provide vital information that will assist you in helping students master collection skills.

> **NOTE:** You may wish to address the needs of students who are reading below grade level. If so, you can administer the Diagnostic Assessment for Reading Intervention, found in the front of *Holt Reading Solutions.* This assessment is designed to identify a student's reading level and to diagnose the specific reading comprehension skills that need instructional attention.

Holt Online Essay Scoring can be used as a diagnostic tool to evaluate students' writing proficiency:

- For each essay, the online scoring system delivers a holistic score and analytic feedback related to five writing traits. These two scoring methods will enable you to pinpoint the strengths of your students' writing as well as skills that need improvement.

Ongoing, Informal Assessment

The **Student Edition** offers systematic opportunities for ongoing, informal assessment and immediate instructional follow-up. Students' responses to their reading; their writing, listening, and speaking projects; and their work with vocabulary skills all serve as both instructional and ongoing assessment tasks.

vii

FOR THE TEACHER

Overview of ELEMENTS OF LITERATURE Assessment Program *continued*

- Throughout the **Student Edition,** practice and assessment are immediate and occur at the point where skills are taught.

- In order for assessment to inform instruction on an ongoing basis, related material repeats instruction and then offers new opportunities for informal assessment.

- **Skills Reviews** at the end of each collection offer a quick evaluation of how well students have mastered the collection skills.

Progress Assessment

Students' mastery of the content of the **Student Edition** is systematically assessed in two test booklets:

- *Holt Assessment: Literature, Reading, and Vocabulary* offers a test for every selection. Multiple-choice questions focus on comprehension, the selected skills, and vocabulary development. In addition, students write answers to constructed-response prompts that test their understanding of the skills.

- *Holt Assessment: Writing, Listening, and Speaking* provides both multiple-choice questions for writing and analytical scales and rubrics for writing, listening, and speaking. These instruments assess proficiency in all the writing applications appropriate for each grade level.

Summative Assessment

Holt Assessment: Literature, Reading, and Vocabulary contains two types of summative tests:

- The Collection Summative Tests, which appear at the end of every collection, ask students to apply their recently acquired skills to a new literary selection. These tests contain both multiple-choice questions and constructed-response prompts.

- The End-of-Year Test helps you determine how well students have mastered the skills and concepts taught during the year. This test mirrors the Entry-Level Test and uses multiple tasks to assess mastery of literary, reading, and vocabulary skills.

FOR THE TEACHER

Overview of ELEMENTS OF LITERATURE Assessment Program *continued*

Holt Online Essay Scoring can be used as an end-of-year assessment tool:

- You can use *Holt Online Essay Scoring* to evaluate how well students have mastered the writing skills taught during the year. You will be able to assess student mastery using a holistic score as well as analytic feedback based on five writing traits.

Monitoring Student Progress

Both *Holt Assessment: Literature, Reading, and Vocabulary* and *Holt Assessment: Writing, Listening, and Speaking* include skills profiles that record progress toward the mastery of skills. Students and teachers can use the profiles to monitor student progress.

One-Stop Planner® CD-ROM with ExamView® Test Generator

All of the questions in this booklet are available on the *One-Stop Planner® CD-ROM with ExamView® Test Generator*. You can use the ExamView Test Generator to customize any of the tests in this booklet. You can then print a test unique to your classroom situation.

Holt Online Assessment

You can use *Holt Online Assessment* to administer and score the diagnostic and summative tests online. You can then generate and print reports to document student growth and class results. For your students, this online resource provides individual assessment of strengths and weaknesses and immediate feedback.

FOR THE TEACHER
About This Book

This book, *Holt Assessment: Writing, Listening, and Speaking*, accompanies the ELEMENTS OF LITERATURE program and provides a variety of assessment resources. These include Writing Workshop Tests and Answer Key, Workshop Scales and Rubrics, Scales and Sample Papers, and Portfolio Assessment.

WRITING WORKSHOP TESTS AND ANSWER KEY

Every Writing Workshop in ELEMENTS OF LITERATURE has an accompanying Writing Workshop Test in a standardized test format. The test format not only will allow you to assess student performance but also will familiarize students with standardized tests and give them experience in test taking.

Each Writing Workshop Test provides a passage containing problems or errors in several or all of the following areas: content, organization, style, and conventions. Students demonstrate their understanding of the writing genre and their revising and proofreading skills by responding to multiple-choice items. Students revise elements of the genre, restructure segments of the passage, add or delete statements, refine language, and correct errors in the passage.

Answer Sheets

Answer Sheets immediately follow the tests in this section. The Answer Sheets correspond to the answer options on a particular standardized test. Use the following chart to help you determine which answer sheet to use.

Workshop	Answer Sheet
Writing Workshops for Collections 1–3 and 5–6	Answer Sheet 1
Writing Workshop for Collection 4	Answer Sheet 2

Answer Key

The Answer Key follows the Answer Sheets at the end of this section of the book. In addition to giving the correct answer, the Answer Key tells which Workshop skill is assessed by each item.

FOR THE TEACHER

About This Book *continued*

WORKSHOP SCALES AND RUBRICS

This section contains analytical scales and scoring rubrics for Writing Workshops and scales for Listening and Speaking Workshops. Both the scales and the rubrics are important teacher evaluation tools. In addition, students can use the scales and rubrics as learning and evaluation guides for their own work.

The **scales** include essential criteria for mastery of skills and ratings of each criterion based on a four-point scale. The **rubrics** are based on the same criteria listed in the scales. The rubrics clearly describe a student's work at each score point level for each specific criterion.

Score Point 0

On occasion, student work may be unscorable and consequently will receive a score point of zero. This may be true of writing, listening and speaking, and media assignments. The following are reasons to give a product a score of zero. The work

- is not relevant to the prompt or assignment
- is only a rewording of the prompt or assignment
- contains an insufficient amount of writing (or other mode) to determine whether it addresses the prompt or assignment
- is a copy of previously published work
- is illegible, incomprehensible, blank, or in a language other than English

FOR THE TEACHER

About This Book *continued*

SCALES AND SAMPLE PAPERS

This section contains two different kinds of scales for assessing writing: the Analytical Scale: 7 Writing Traits and the individual four-point holistic scales for fictional or autobiographical writing, exposition, responses to literature, persuasion, and business letters. Accompanying these scales are high-level, mid-level, and low-level examples of student writing. Individual evaluations, based on the analytical and holistic scales, follow each sample student paper. These scales can be used for on-demand writing or class assignments. Although this section is directed to teachers, students may also benefit from access to this section as they write and revise.

PORTFOLIO ASSESSMENT

This section provides an introduction to portfolio work, including suggestions about how to develop and use portfolios and how to conduct conferences with students about their work.

Forms

The introductory article is followed by a set of student forms for assessing and organizing portfolio contents and for setting goals for future work. Also included is a set of forms for communicating with parents or guardians about student work and for generally assessing students' progress.

Forms in this section can be used to record work, to establish baselines and goals, and to think critically about student work in a variety of areas. These areas include writing, listening, and speaking. The goal of these forms is to encourage students to develop criteria for assessing their own work and to identify areas for improvement. Many forms can also be used for assessment of a peer's work and for teacher evaluations.

Writing Workshop Tests and Answer Key

Writing Workshop: Editorial

for COLLECTION 1 page 138

DIRECTIONS Janis is writing an editorial for her school newspaper. She wants to promote increased awareness of severe food allergies by engaging her audience and gaining their support. Read the draft of the editorial and answer items 1 through 10.

Food for Thought

Simple, common foods can cause complex and severe medical problems. (1) In New York, a 17-year-old high school student passed away after having (2) an allergic reaction to peanuts in a snack mix. The young woman was at (3) a party, ate the mix, and began to have trouble breathing. Her symptoms (4) worsened, and she died at the hospital a short time later. Food allergies (5) affect more than six million people in the United States. Furthermore, teens (6) are the highest-risk group for severe food-allergy reactions. All teens and (7) school personnel need to be aware of this very real danger.

Reactions frequently occur when a young adult is away from home. (8) Too often adolescents are not prepared for how fast a reaction can (9) happen—in some cases, mere minutes. The most severe type of allergic (10) reaction, anaphylaxis (a reaction resulting in shock or other adverse physical response), can be sudden.

Greater awareness of food allergies is crucial because eight common (11) food types cause 90 percent of all allergic reactions. Serious reactions can (12) occur from a mere trace of these foods. There is no cure for food allergies— (13) the only way to prevent an allergic reaction is strict avoidance of the allergy-causing food.

Food allergies can have a serious emotional, as well as physical, impact. (14) Affected teens and their families say they live with constant fear of a severe (15) reaction. They also find it very difficult to avoid common foods such as (16) peanuts, eggs, and milk if these are the foods to which they are sensitive. Although teens may be aware of their food sensitivity, they may still eat (17)

GO ON

Writing Workshop Tests 3

EDITORIAL

the food, unaware of its presence in a dish, and have a reaction. This uncertainty really takes a toll on teens and their families. Simple things like visiting relatives, going on field trips, or eating food at parties can turn into dangerous situations. Teens with food allergies say avoiding all traces of certain foods is stressful and difficult, especially when the food, like peanut oil, for example, is not easily visible in a dish. At cafeterias, restaurants, and parties, it may be hard to know if an allergen is present in certain prepared foods.

Students can recognize symptoms and learn what to do in an emergency. School nurses can be informed about individual students' allergies so they can administer medication quickly. Certain foods should not be served by the cafeteria staff. All school personnel can be trained to manage situations in which the severely allergic teen begins to react to a food.

Food allergies can be life threatening, and reactions can come on very quickly. The stress of ongoing worry about accidental exposure to foods can be reduced in the school setting. Students' lives can be saved if school personnel know about the problem of severe food allergies. Wouldn't it be wise to take time to learn about food allergies? A safe environment and informed teens will go a long way toward preventing severe reactions in students with food allergies.

(Sentence numbers: 18, 19, 20, 21, 22, 23, 24, 25, 26, 27, 28, 29, 30)

1 Which of these, if added to the beginning of sentence 1, would BEST grab readers' attention?

A As you may have heard
B How have you learned that
C Did you know that
D Because you understand

2 Which is the BEST change to make to sentence 2 to avoid a euphemism?

A Replace "New York" with "a state in the Northeast."
B Replace "snack mix" with "a mixture of snack foods."
C Replace "passed away" with "died."
D Replace "17-year-old high school student" with "high school senior."

GO ON

4 Holt Assessment: Writing, Listening, and Speaking

3 Which phrase, if added to the end of sentence 7, would BEST clarify the opinion statement?

A and tell family members
B and know a doctor
C and call on the phone
D and know what to do

4 Which of the following should be added to paragraph 2 as the BEST statement of the reason discussed in that paragraph?

A Teens with food allergies should not be away from home.
B Teens are responsible for allergic reactions.
C Severe allergic reactions can happen quickly and cause significant problems.
D Avoid allergic reactions by eating only a few foods.

5 What should be added to sentence 10 to state an important piece of evidence?

A but is not significant
B and life threatening
C and can cause breakouts
D but can be ignored

6 What supporting evidence could BEST be added after sentence 11?

A These include common foods like eggs, nuts, and shellfish.
B These are the most common food allergens.
C These foods are available in your local grocery store.
D Common foods can cause surprising medical complications.

7 Which of the following sentences should begin paragraph 5 in order to clearly state the reason discussed in the paragraph?

A Finally, informing school personnel about allergic reactions might make the difference between life and death for some students.
B Finally, parents of teens with severe food allergies should try to reduce their children's stress and anxiety.
C Finally, homeroom teachers and study hall monitors need to be informed about any severe food allergies students may have.
D Finally, teens with severe food allergies need to wear medical tags with the name of the food they have to avoid.

8 What change should be made to sentence 24 to create a series of parallel sentences?

A Also, certain foods should be avoided in the cafeteria.
B Cafeteria staff can be alerted not to serve certain foods.
C Someone needs to tell the cafeteria staff about this problem.
D Teens with allergies should bring their lunches from home.

EDITORIAL

9 Which of the following sentences would be the BEST restatement of the opinion to add to the conclusion?

- A Students with food allergies need help.
- B Parents have all of the responsibility for making their environments safe for students with food allergies.
- C Students with food allergies are responsible for their own well-being.
- D It is extremely important for students and all school staff to be informed and aware of severe food allergies.

10 Which is the BEST replacement, if any, for sentence 30 to end with a call to action?

- A It is possible for students and teachers to help by talking about the situation.
- B Should students and schools help with this problem?
- C School boards should establish a policy for education and increased awareness of food allergies.
- D Leave as is.

for COLLECTION 2 — page 338

Writing Workshop: Short Story

DIRECTIONS The following is a rough draft of a short story about two people who approach a new task very differently. It may contain errors in development and organization. Some of the questions may refer to numbered sentences within the text. Read the story and answer questions 1 through 10.

First Bath

"Sooner or later, we've got to give him a bath." (1) He met her serious eyes and turned to look tenderly at the compact little (2) body nestled in its blanket on the couch between them. "But he's sleeping. (3) He looks so peaceful. Do we have to do it *now*?" (4) (5)

"We've put it off long enough. He's getting pretty grubby, you'll admit." (6) (7) "Ok, Ok, Ann; you'll keep pestering me until I agree. Should I get the (8) (9) book?"

"Look, Ray, I've seen this done lots of times. Get the book if you insist, (10) (11) but we are two reasonably competent human beings, and I know *I* don't need some how-to book in order to get him clean." Ann stood up, scooped (12) the sleepy bundle into her arms, and marched into the tiny bathroom. Ray (13) crowded in behind her and opened the book he was carrying.

"The book says the water should be lukewarm. Test it on your wrist." (14) (15) "Ray, the water's fine! Would you stop worrying about everything and (16) (17) help me unwrap him?" Irritated but trying to cooperate, they unwound the (18) soft blue blanket, and Ann gently lowered the little body into the tub.

"So far, so good. No! Wait a minute!" Ray found a page he had marked. (19) (20) (21) "This says to be sure to keep his head up." (22)

"I *am* keeping his head up! Will you quit giving me obvious advice?" (23) (24)

"His head's under the water—you're *drowning* him!" (25)

Ann was furious. "I am *not* drowning him. I am giving him a *bath*. (26) (27) (28) He has to get *wet* to have a bath. Bath—wet: They go together." (29) (30)

GO ON

Writing Workshop Tests **7**

for **COLLECTION 2** continued

SHORT STORY

Ray ran his finger down the page. "Next, you—," but a sudden splash
(31)   (32)
cut him off. Ray's head jerked to attention. Ann was completely soaked.
     (33)   (34)
"Now for the rinse." This time Ann's cold stare stopped him midsentence.
(35)   (36)

She didn't speak, but her movements showed how fed up she was.
         (37)

"What now?" Ray asked, knowing Ann was out of patience with him.
  (38)

"Just a minute. Watch the little one." Ann leaned over the edge of the
  (39)   (40)   (41)
tub to pull the plug.

Before she could turn around again, the little body shuddered and
      (42)
shook mightily, shedding every last drop of water from the golden fur.
The walls, the floor, the rug, the mirror—and Ray—were wet.
(43)

Peering through his dripping glasses, Ray exclaimed, "What a mess!"
   (44)
Ray wondered if he should find another towel.
(45)

"Yes. It is, isn't it?" said Ann, calmly. She wrapped the puppy in a towel
 (46)   (47)
and walked into the kitchen. A minute later her head appeared again in
                    (48)
the bathroom doorway, and she spoke her last words on the subject.

1 Which revision, if any, should be made in sentence 2?

A Replace *He* with *Ray* and *her* with *Ann's*.

B Replace *the compact little body* with the name of the pet.

C Tell the reader what Ann and Ray look like.

D Leave as is.

2 Which line of dialogue, if added after sentence 8, would help establish the conflict in the story?

A "At least he isn't too smelly yet."

B "But are you sure you know what you're doing?"

C "Be sure to call me if you need any help."

D "I read about baths in that book we have."

GO ON

8 Holt Assessment: Writing, Listening, and Speaking

for COLLECTION 2 continued

SHORT STORY

3 Which is the BEST replacement for *opened* in sentence 13?

- A flipped to a dog-eared page in
- B quickly showed her
- C started to read aloud from
- D found the subject he was looking for in

4 Which line of dialogue should be added after sentence 21 to further develop the conflict?

- A "I can show you the page where this is discussed."
- B "Should I now be holding him?"
- C "Don't let his head flop that way."
- D "Have you practiced this before?"

5 Which sentence should be added before sentence 25 to continue the development of the plot complications?

- A Ray was really nervous about this first bath.
- B Ray wanted Ann to stop what she was doing and read the book.
- C Ray heard a snort from the bathtub.
- D Ray continued to argue with Ann.

6 Which is the BEST revision of sentence 26?

- A Ann was clearly upset, and Ray could hardly hear her.
- B Ann seemed really angry and frustrated.
- C Ann closed her mouth and mumbled softly.
- D Ann's teeth were clenched tightly, and she spoke quickly.

7 Which sentence would be the BEST replacement for sentence 34?

- A A lot of water had splashed on Ann, and she was soaking wet.
- B Water was streaming from Ann's hair, and a big drop rolled off the end of her nose.
- C Ann was soaked, but Ray decided to ignore her.
- D Water was streaming down Ann's face, neck, and arms.

8 Which revision of sentence 37 would BEST describe Ann's anger?

- A She grabbed a towel and pulled the moving body from the tub.
- B Turning her back so Ray wouldn't see her anger, Ann lifted the little body from the tub.
- C Getting a towel, Ann raised the moving body from the tub and set it at Ray's feet.
- D Ann snapped a towel off the bar, hoisted the wriggling body from the tub, and thrust it at Ray.

9 Which is the BEST replacement for *wet* in sentence 43 to create a figure of speech?

- A moist and totally fogged up
- B dripping like a tree in the rain
- C covered with huge drops of water
- D slippery and hopelessly messed up

10 Which is the BEST line of dialogue to add after sentence 48 to conclude the story?

- A "I think it's your turn to clean up this messy place."
- B "I hope your book got wet, too!"
- C "You'd better see what your book says about cleaning up the bathroom."
- D "I don't want to see that book again."

Writing Workshop Tests **9**

for **COLLECTION 3** page 426

Writing Workshop: Reflective Essay

DIRECTIONS Diana is writing a reflective essay about a significant experience in her life. She has decided to write about running her first marathon. Read Diana's essay and answer questions 1 through 10.

A Marathon Achievement

"I think this marathon begins too early," was my nervous reaction as
(1)
I eyed the starting line. It was a crisp February day and one for which I had
(2)
trained for the past six months—the start of my first marathon. The starting
(3)
area was awash with activity as excited runners clad in spandex and
T-shirts stretched, visited with friends, or chomped on a last-minute bagel
carbohydrate boost. Loud rock music pounded. The beginning of the
(4)   (5)
marathon was filled with anticipation.

   The starting gun blasted and waves of runners bolted through the gate.
(6)
I joined the colorful sea of runners that steadily pounded the pavement in
(7)
a comfortable jog. The early morning was chilly, but I peeled off my black-
(8)
and-white windbreaker at the second mile. The next four miles went by
(9)
in a blur of scenery, well-wishers, and water stations. At the 6.2-mile mark,
(10)
I was pleasantly surprised to feel really strong. I never dreamed I could run
(11)
this far, much less be aiming for twenty more miles. I also got a tremen-
(12)
dous boost from my family, who had traveled from the starting gate to
the 6.2-mile mark to cheer for me. I sped by, recharged for more miles.
(13)
   Alongside me ran fatigue-clad buddies from a local military base chant-
(14)
ing army ditties: "I do what I've been told. Running hard in the cold! Army
life is only for the bold!" Besides the musical military, runners were all
(15)
shapes and sizes and from all walks of life.

   At mile 13, a little over two hours for me, we heard that the first elite
(16)
runners had finished. Though I envied their speed, I was pleased that I
(17)

GO ON

was still in the race. However, around mile 15, I started feeling a bit tired (18) and worried. I had heard horror stories of long-distance runners who hit (19) a "wall" in agony and can go no further. I definitely did not want to be (20) one of those statistics, especially after months of giving up my Saturday mornings and dealing with aching hamstrings.

After mile 18, the marathon became a test of will. I wondered if most (21) (22) of the runners were holding up. My legs felt like concrete blocks, my feet (23) were on fire, and my body screamed to stop. I was slowing down, but run, (24) walk, or crawl, I was going to finish. The mile-25 marker beckoned me to (25) the finish, but every muscle in my body ached. Every step was an effort, (26) and every breath an incredible labor.

I witnessed the garish yellow clock and archway signaling the end of (27) this athletic torture. A feeling of exhilaration hit me as I crossed that finish (28) line. I had done it—26.2 miles! Swept up in the emotion of the moment, (29) (30) I had a powerful realization.

1. How should the quotation at the beginning of sentence 1 be changed for the MOST engaging opening?

A "Maybe another time,"
B "What WAS I thinking?"
C "A lot of runners are here,"
D "I probably should go home,"

2. Which clause, if added to the end of sentence 1, would provide the BEST descriptive details?

A which was marked by colorful displays of balloons
B which had just been set up that morning by the staff
C which began to seem like a goal in itself
D which was tied with bright red, white, and blue balloons

NAME _____ CLASS _____ DATE _____

for COLLECTION 3 continued   **REFLECTIVE ESSAY**

3 Which sentence if added to the introduction would BEST hint at the significance of the experience?

A I learned that running a marathon is loud and exhausting.

B Proper training is the key for anyone who wants to run a marathon.

C I knew I wouldn't win the race, but the end had its own surprise.

D Avoid marathons whenever possible.

4 How could the beginning of sentence 7 BEST be revised to provide narrative details?

A Someone yelled at me as

B "I can do this," I whispered to myself, as

C The marathon was a favorite local event, as

D "This is tough but possible," one man said, as

5 What is the BEST narrative detail to add to the beginning of sentence 11?

A Growing up as an awkward, non-athletic kid,

B Since I had not known any runners before,

C Not much interested in distances,

D Because I prefer to drive or ride in a car,

6 What narrative detail could BEST be added after sentence 15?

A These include runners, joggers, and walkers.

B These are the most common runners.

C The oldest was in his eighties, the youngest was only twelve.

D The runners race in local events.

7 Which paragraph, if any, should be moved to clarify the order of events?

A 1

B 2

C 3

D Leave as is.

8 What is the BEST revision, if any, of sentence 27 to make it sound more natural?

A I witnessed the imposing yellow clock and archway.

B I observed the garish yellow clock and archway at the end of the race.

C I saw the gaudy yellow clock and archway signaling the end of the race.

D Leave as is.

9 What should be added to the conclusion to make a connection between the experience and life in general?

A Running a marathon is not about the athleticism, but about believing in yourself.

B Does any reward—even winning an event—really match the effort?

C Marathons are simple events, but they can create a great sense of empathy with fellow runners.

D Running a marathon is best left to athletes and the ambitious.

10 Which of the following would be the BEST statement of the significance of the experience?

A Everyone needs to make the effort.

B For me, it's about going the distance.

C If at first you don't succeed, just try again.

D No pain, no gain.

Writing Workshop: Reporting Historical Research

DIRECTIONS Sean is writing a research paper on the building of the Hoover Dam. His research question is *What made the Hoover Dam the most amazing engineering accomplishment of its time?* Read Sean's draft and answer questions 1 through 15.

Note: Sean has not yet included page numbers for his sources.

Hoover Dam: Conquering the Mighty Colorado River

Hoover Dam, sometimes referred to as Boulder Dam, was constructed (1) between 1931 and 1935 to harness the waters of the wild Colorado River. The dam was a challenging task for even the most experienced profession-(2) als. Many have called Hoover Dam a wonder of the modern world (3) because of its unprecedented massive size and its designers' ingenuity in overcoming obstacles that were considered impossible barriers at the time (Stevens).

Hoover Dam is 726.4 feet high, more than twice the height of the highest (4) dam built before it. It is 1,244 feet across the top and 660 feet thick at the (5) bottom. It weighs 6.6 million tons and contains more than 3.25 million (6) cubic yards of concrete ("Hoover Dam"). Hoover Dam set the precedent (7) for modern dam-building technology, though there are higher and more massive dams today.

The engineers who designed Hoover Dam came up with ingenious (8) solutions to the problems of building such a massive concrete structure. For example, they first had to figure out how to force the river to flow (9) around the construction site. To solve this problem they built four huge (10) diversion tunnels to take the water through the canyon walls while they were building the dam. Another seemingly insurmountable problem was (11) that the concrete would have taken over a century to cool completely if it had been poured in one huge form. To overcome this, the engineers came (12) up with a building-block system and a network of cooling tubes to speed

the process. Engineers also invented a complex system of cables and pul-
(13)
leys to transport materials and workers up and down the sides of the
canyon and across the face of the dam. These and other innovations are
(14)
reasons why Hoover Dam still stands as a monument to human ingenuity
("Hoover Dam").

   Along with being massive and ingenious in its construction, Hoover
(15)
Dam was also built in an amazingly short period of time. More than 5,000
(16)
men found jobs during the Great Depression working on the dam. Ila
(17)
Clements-Davey, a dam worker's daughter, said, "The men were just
swarming over the whole place, they just looked like a hill of ants"
(<u>The American Experience</u>). However, working conditions were harsh.
(18)

   It was a brutal job under the best of circumstances. But the
   summer of 1931 was one of the hottest on record. The men
   worked in blistering heat without shade or adequate drinking
   water. Workers collapsed from the heat. . . . (<u>The American
   Experience</u>).

Shifts were long. Carbon monoxide poisoning from the trucks' exhaust
(19)   (20)
fumes was common. Falls from the canyon walls and other work-related
(21)
accidents were unfortunately common as well. Workers were paid $4.00
(22)
per day. Work never stopped on the dam—the men worked in three shifts,
(23)
around the clock, to complete the job on time (<u>The American Experience</u>).
Not only did they complete it on time, but they beat the government's
(24)
deadline by more than two years!

   The energy harnessed behind the dam provided power to the
(25)
populations of Arizona, Nevada, and California, and the water of the newly
formed Lake Mead would provide fresh water and irrigation for the same
region ("Story of Hoover Dam"). Human beings had conquered the mighty
(26)
Colorado, which had flowed unchecked and wild for millions of years.

President Herbert Hoover, for whom the dam was named, summed up (27) the achievement in these words:

> Civilization advances with the practical application of knowledge in such structures as the one being built here in the pathway of one of the great rivers of the continent. The spread of its values in human happiness is beyond computation.

Hoover Dam is an amazing example of how humans harness the forces (28) of nature.

Works Cited

<u>The American Experience: Hoover Dam.</u> Dir. Stephen Stept. Videocassette. PBS Video, 1999.

"Herbert Hoover and the Colorado River." <u>Hoover Dam.</u> U.S. Department of the Interior, Bureau of Reclamation. 16 April 2002. <http://www.hooverdam.com/History/hhoover.html>.

"The Story of Hoover Dam." <u>Hoover Dam.</u> U.S. Department of the Interior, Bureau of Reclamation. 16 April 2002. <http://www.hooverdam.usbr.gov/History/index.htm>.

"Hoover Dam: Source of the American West's Oasis Civilization." <u>SunsetCities.com.</u> 16 June 2002. <http://www.sunsetcities.com/hoover-dam.html>.

Stevens, Joseph E. <u>Hoover Dam: An American Adventure.</u> Norman and London: University of Oklahoma Press, 1988.

for COLLECTION 4 continued

REPORTING HISTORICAL RESEARCH

1 Which of the following would BEST and most appropriately draw the readers in if inserted before sentence 1?

  A It was bigger than the Statue of Liberty.

  B How was Hoover Dam built? That is what this paper is going to explain.

  C People told many stories about building Hoover Dam, and most of them can be proved true.

  D Did you know that Hoover Dam was named after President Herbert Hoover?

2 Which sentence, if added after sentence 2, would give readers the BEST overview of the research and main ideas?

  A It was the biggest thing anyone had ever seen, and Americans were thrilled to have built it.

  B It was more expensive than any other public project that had ever been built before in the United States, but cost was beside the point where Hoover Dam was concerned.

  C It was constructed in a surprisingly short period of time under harsh conditions; and it tamed the mighty Colorado.

  D Many new devices had to be invented to achieve its construction, such as the drilling jumbo and a cooling system to harden the concrete.

3 Which is the BEST thesis statement to add to the introduction?

  A The Hoover Dam is so large it attracts tourists from all over the world.

  B The dam was the most significant engineering feat of its time and changed life in the Southwest.

  C Workers were eager to participate in the construction of the dam because jobs were hard to get during the Great Depression.

  D Engineers had to work nonstop in order to create a large dam so quickly.

4 Which is the BEST revision of sentence 7 to provide variety and prevent it from being too similar to the structure of the other sentences in the paragraph?

  A It is no longer the country's highest or most massive dam, but Hoover Dam set the precedent for modern dam-building technology.

  B There are higher and more massive dams today, but Hoover Dam set the precedent for modern dam-building technology.

  C Though there are higher and more massive dams today, Hoover Dam set the precedent for modern dam-building technology.

  D Leave as is.

for **COLLECTION 4** continued

REPORTING HISTORICAL RESEARCH

5 Refer to Sean's research question to determine which of the following topics would be the BEST additional main idea.

A how the Hoover Dam was named by government leaders

B explanation of the job of "high-scalers," who worked suspended from high canyon walls

C the political process of getting the dam project approved and funded

D the artworks that enhance the appearance of the dam and the visitors' center

6 Which sentence represents the BEST elaboration to insert after sentence 6?

A It makes one feel tiny to stand at the base of the dam.

B Hoover Dam attracts thousands of tourists every year, generating millions of dollars for the state of Nevada.

C In fact, it was the first single structure to contain more masonry than the Great Pyramid at Giza.

D However, the Grand Coulee Dam in Washington dwarfs the Hoover Dam with its sheer mass.

7 Which sentence should be deleted because it does not directly support the point of the fourth paragraph?

A sentence 17
B sentence 18
C sentence 22
D sentence 24

8 What summary might BEST replace the long quotation in the fourth paragraph?

A It was extremely hot.

B The men were proud to be working on the dam, even during the summer of 1931.

C The men wanted hats and ice water to help them endure the heat.

D Temperatures soared in the summer of 1931, and many men became severely ill.

9 What is the BEST way to revise sentence 23 to add variety to sentence beginnings?

A The men worked in three shifts, around the clock, and because work never stopped, the job was completed on time.

B Because work never stopped on the dam—the men worked in three shifts, around the clock—the job was completed on time.

C The job was completed on time because work never stopped—the men worked in three shifts, around the clock.

D The men completed the job on time by working in three shifts, around the clock, so work never stopped.

GO ON

for COLLECTION 4 *continued*   **REPORTING HISTORICAL RESEARCH**

10. Which of the following would be the BEST elaboration to insert after sentence 25?

A. Many people missed the uncontrolled and unpredictable nature of the Colorado River.

B. Lake Mead became a popular fishing spot for local sports enthusiasts.

C. Moreover, the residents and farmers of the valleys would no longer have to fear river floods.

D. Energy from the Hoover Dam supplied weapons factories during World War II.

11. Where does Sean MOST need to insert a parenthetical citation?

A. after sentence 24

B. after sentence 26

C. at the end of the fourth paragraph

D. after the long quotation in the last paragraph

12. What is the BEST way to summarize the main points of the paper for the conclusion?

A. Hoover Dam was the most amazing engineering accomplishment of its time.

B. Hoover Dam was an amazing accomplishment because of its size, the speed of its construction, and the impact it had on life in the Southwest.

C. Anyone who sees Hoover Dam in person can't help but be awed by its size and its strength.

D. President Hoover would be so proud to see the dam today, still holding back the mighty Colorado and providing power to the desert.

13. Which addition at the end of sentence 28 would BEST restate the thesis?

A. by using brute force and determination to win at any cost.

B. through sheer determination and hard work.

C. by engineering ingenious structures that provide greater quality of life.

D. while employing thousands of workers.

14. Which of the following would be the BEST thought-provoking idea to conclude the paper?

A. During the 1930s, no one thought the Hoover Dam could be built. What "impossible" task will we accomplish next?

B. I hope to be able to visit the Hoover Dam in person some day.

C. What do you think makes the Hoover Dam such an enduring symbol of human ingenuity?

D. Think about this—what if the Hoover Dam had never been built?

15. Which, if any, change should be made to Works Cited?

A. Use alphabetical order.

B. Underline book titles.

C. Delete the Web site addresses.

D. Leave as is.

18   Holt Assessment: Writing, Listening, and Speaking

Writing Workshop: Analyzing a Novel

DIRECTIONS Jared wrote this rough draft of an analysis of a novel. It may contain errors in organization and development. Read the literary analysis and answer questions 1 through 10.

Note: Jared has not yet provided the citations for quotations from the novel.

On the River: Natural Goodness in *Adventures of Huckleberry Finn*

The *Adventures of Huckleberry Finn* chronicles the Mississippi River (1) journey of two runaways—the title character and Jim, a man who is escaping slavery. (2) The novel examines the theme of nature versus civilization. (3) Huck Finn is a natural, down-to-earth character who feels separated from society. (4) Widow Douglas is trying to "sivilize" Huck, and he blames himself for being "so ignorant and so kind of low-down and ornery." (5) Twain shows that Huck's naturalness is redeeming.

Twain illustrates the superiority of nature over civilization through (6) Huck and Jim's life together on the raft. (7) Huck has been raised to consider Jim inferior to himself, and his social conscience, which symbolizes civilization, tells him that "people would call me a low-down Ablitionist" for not turning Jim in to the authorities. (8) Huck overcomes his acquired prejudice, however; his decision to help Jim shows his natural concern for another human being and his innate respect for human dignity. (9) Huck and Jim live peacefully and cooperatively on the raft, floating down the river. "Jim, this is nice . . . I wouldn't want to be nowhere else but here. (10) Pass me (11) along another hunk of fish."

When the action of the novel takes place on land (a symbol of civiliza-(12)tion), the atmosphere changes. For example, while Huck is staying with the (13) Grangerford family, the family's long-standing feud with the Shepherdsons escalates and ends in slaughter. Unlike the negative aspects of civilization (14) on land, life on the river is helpful and compassionate, for "[i]t would a been a miserable business to have any unfriendliness on the raft." . . .

"What you want, above all things, on a raft, is for everybody to be satisfied, (15) and feel right and kind toward the others." Huck's statement reveals (16) Twain's own view that life on the river is natural and innately good, as are Huck's natural instincts toward Jim.

Early in the novel, the mighty Mississippi River is established as a major (17) symbol of the natural world and what it provides. The river offers Huck a means of escape from his father: "I went along up the bank with one eye (18) out for pap and t'other one out for what the rise might fetch along" and (19) "all at once, here comes a canoe; just a beauty, too." Later, the river (20) provides a raft and supplies for Huck and Jim to begin their journey.

The novel's conclusion shows that the river journey with Jim has (21) allowed Huck's natural self to, in part, defeat civilization's negative pull on him. The novel ends with Huck planning to "light out for the [Western] (22) Territory ahead of the rest" because another woman wants to adopt and "sivilize" him, and he "can't stand it."

Twain uses the river journey to show the struggle between the demands (23) of civilized society and the instinctive goodness of the natural world. Huck wrestles to the end with the war between his conscience and society's (24) requirements. Finally, we see, along with Huck, that he is most comfortable (25) when he is on the actual, as well as the metaphorical, river.

1 What addition, if any, should be made to the first sentence of the essay?

- A Insert **The book** before *Adventures*.
- B Insert **Mark Twain's** before *Adventures*.
- C Insert **The great American novel** before *Adventures*.
- D Leave as is.

2 Which is the BEST revision, if any, of the first sentence?

- A Change **the title character** to **Huck, a boy who is running from his abusive father**.
- B Change **the title character** to **a boy called Huck Finn**.
- C Change **the title character** to **one of them running from his abusive father**.
- D Leave as is.

for **COLLECTION 5** continued

ANALYZING A NOVEL

3 Which addition to sentence 5 would BEST clarify the thesis statement?

A and Huck is being too hard on himself

B and disagrees with Huck's self-criticism

C and civilized life will enhance Huck's naturalness

D and his harsh criticism of himself is really a criticism of society

4 In sentence 10, how should the quotation be introduced?

A In Huck's view,

B Huck also says,

C Everyone's happiness on a raft is important:

D As Huck sums it up,

5 In paragraph 3, what evidence should the writer add before sentence 13?

A On land, Huck and Jim encounter violence.

B Huck tries to believe that society is essentially civilized.

C On the river, events are happier, and nature is friendly.

D Huck and Jim meet many people who live along the banks of the river.

6 Before sentence 14, which addition would provide the BEST elaboration of the paragraph's major point?

A A feud like the Grangerford-Shepherdson's is rare.

B The Grangerford-Shepherdson feud provides comfort to Huck and Jim.

C Events like the feud provide a contrast to life on the river.

D People don't kill each other on the river.

7 How should the paragraphs be rearranged, if at all, so that the major points will be logically organized?

A Move the fourth paragraph to follow the first paragraph.

B Move the fourth paragraph to follow the second paragraph.

C Move the second paragraph to follow the fourth paragraph.

D Leave as is.

8 What elaboration would BEST be inserted after sentence 20?

A It is also important in the lives of all the people along its banks.

B It is the source of both physical and psychological good.

C It represents nature, while the town represents hostile civilization.

D It plays an important role in many of Twain's works.

9 Which sentence should be inserted after sentence 21?

A He can no longer accept the conflicts and contradictions of society.

B He has to leave in order to keep exploring nature.

C He sees that the respectable people in town want to control him.

D He understands that slavery is unjust and wrong.

10 Which words should be added after *when he is* in the final sentence?

A remembering the trip with Jim

B fishing and whistling

C following his natural instincts

D enjoying life as he knows it

Writing Workshop Tests **21**

Media Workshop: Analyzing and Using Media

DIRECTIONS Sam is preparing a media presentation on the subject of rescue dogs. He wants to incorporate different types of media to engage his audience and support the text. Read Sam's thesis statement and outline and answer items 1 through 10.

Rescue Dogs: Saving Lives Is All in a Day's Work

Thesis statement: Search-and-rescue dogs are invaluable helpers and savers of lives.

I. Lighthearted introduction of rescue dogs

[Play audiotape of the chorus of the song "Who Let the Dogs Out" by Baha Men, copyright 2000 S-Curve Records.]

II. Rescue dog

[Show series of still photos—rescue dogs in action. Include Saint Bernard in Alps and golden retriever in city]

A. Help people who are trapped or lost—in earthquakes, avalanches, or damaged buildings

B. Look for missing persons, including children and the elderly who become confused and lose their bearings

C. Work with police at crime scenes searching for victims and criminals

III. History of rescue dogs

[Play audio clip of dog barking, follow with slide of dog and a WWII rescue team with caption. Finish section with a modern-day video clip of a rescue dog searching in a crumbled building.]

A. Early Alpine rescues and avalanche searches

B. Military service during the last century

C. Duty in times of trouble all over the world

IV. Characteristics of rescue dogs

[Show photos of individual dogs—Annie, Bailey, Nikko, and Riley—graphics from FBI Kids Web site.]

A. Persevering for long hours under adverse conditions, often toiling without rest

B. Skilled at sniffing out and finding what they are looking for, even underground or underwater

C. Active, energetic dogs

D. Friendly, risk-takers

E. Obsessive and persistent regarding toys

V. Selection and training of rescue dogs

[Show clip of video of dogs in training with handlers; alternate with descriptive text of three most successful breeds.]

A. Selection through breed rescue groups and shelters

B. Preference for young dogs, but dogs accepted up to eighteen months

C. Highest success rates with Labradors, golden retrievers, and border collies

D. Time-intensive training

VI. Conclusion

A. Various types of disasters

B. Many innocent victims rescued

C. Lives saved after disasters

1 Which phrase, if added to the end of the thesis statement, would BEST clarify it?

A when they are fed
B and do not rely on people
C and can be famous
D when disaster strikes

2 Which of the following would make the BEST replacement heading for section II?

A Overview of rescue dog activities
B Work mainly in large cities
C Often tired to point of collapse
D Similarities to emergency workers

3 What visual element could be added to BEST illustrate the point made in II. C?

A Photo of rescue dog with little child
B Audio recording of "The Twelve Dogs of Christmas"
C Photo of a German shepherd with police handler
D Illustration of a dog's skeletal structure

4 What should be added to section III as an important point about the history of rescue dogs?

A Rescue dogs featured on television
B Long-standing tradition of rescue dogs
C Common traits of rescue dogs and pet dogs
D Better success of some breeds as rescue dogs

GO ON

Writing Workshop Tests **23**

for COLLECTION 6 continued

USING MEDIA

5. What supporting visual information could be added to illustrate the point in IV. A?

A CD-ROM information on different breeds of dogs
B Illustration of famous TV cartoon dog Scooby Doo
C Slide of dog in difficult training class
D Video clip of dog on a laborious search-and-rescue mission

6. Which section, if any, should be moved to improve the logical order of the presentation?

A I
B III
C IV
D Leave as is.

7. What supporting media could BEST be added to section V?

A Chart of best ages of dogs for training
B Names of famous rescue dogs
C Most popular names for dogs
D Newspaper article about a dog show

8. Which point could BEST be added after V. D?

A Friendly nature of rescue dogs
B Powerful muscles of rescue dogs
C Great expense of training
D Years of work for rescue dogs

9. Which supporting media would be MOST effective for the conclusion?

A Photos of famous dogs known to most moviegoers
B Recordings of several different songs that feature dog subjects
C Graph of increased use of rescue dogs
D Series of TV clips of dogs working in tornado, earthquake, and flood areas

10. What would be the BEST addition to the conclusion?

A Natural or man-made disasters
B Unpaid status of rescue dogs
C Heroism of rescue dogs
D Heroism of emergency workers

24 Holt Assessment: Writing, Listening, and Speaking

NAME _____ CLASS _____ DATE _____ SCORE _____

Answer Sheet 1

Collection _____

Writing Workshop

1. Ⓐ Ⓑ Ⓒ Ⓓ
2. Ⓐ Ⓑ Ⓒ Ⓓ
3. Ⓐ Ⓑ Ⓒ Ⓓ
4. Ⓐ Ⓑ Ⓒ Ⓓ
5. Ⓐ Ⓑ Ⓒ Ⓓ
6. Ⓐ Ⓑ Ⓒ Ⓓ
7. Ⓐ Ⓑ Ⓒ Ⓓ
8. Ⓐ Ⓑ Ⓒ Ⓓ
9. Ⓐ Ⓑ Ⓒ Ⓓ
10. Ⓐ Ⓑ Ⓒ Ⓓ

NAME _____ CLASS _____ DATE _____ SCORE _____

Answer Sheet 2
Collection _____

Writing Workshop

1. Ⓐ Ⓑ Ⓒ Ⓓ   6. Ⓐ Ⓑ Ⓒ Ⓓ   11. Ⓐ Ⓑ Ⓒ Ⓓ
2. Ⓐ Ⓑ Ⓒ Ⓓ   7. Ⓐ Ⓑ Ⓒ Ⓓ   12. Ⓐ Ⓑ Ⓒ Ⓓ
3. Ⓐ Ⓑ Ⓒ Ⓓ   8. Ⓐ Ⓑ Ⓒ Ⓓ   13. Ⓐ Ⓑ Ⓒ Ⓓ
4. Ⓐ Ⓑ Ⓒ Ⓓ   9. Ⓐ Ⓑ Ⓒ Ⓓ   14. Ⓐ Ⓑ Ⓒ Ⓓ
5. Ⓐ Ⓑ Ⓒ Ⓓ   10. Ⓐ Ⓑ Ⓒ Ⓓ   15. Ⓐ Ⓑ Ⓒ Ⓓ

Answer Key

Collection 1

Editorial

p. 3

1. C (attention-grabbing opening)
2. C (rhetorical device)
3. D (opinion statement)
4. C (reason for position)
5. B (evidence)
6. A (evidence)
7. A (reason)
8. B (rhetorical device)
9. D (restatement of opinion)
10. C (call to action)

Collection 2

Short Story

p. 7

1. A (introduce main characters)
2. B (initiate conflict)
3. A (concrete sensory details)
4. C (develop conflict)
5. C (develop plot)
6. D (elaborate character)
7. B (concrete sensory details)
8. D (concrete sensory details)
9. B (figurative language)
10. C (resolution of conflict)

Answer Key (continued)

Collection 3

Reflective Essay

p. 10

1. B (engaging readers' attention)
2. D (descriptive detail)
3. C (significance of experience)
4. B (narrative detail)
5. A (narrative detail)
6. C (descriptive detail)
7. D (order of events)
8. C (natural language)
9. A (connection between experience and life)
10. B (significance of experience)

Collection 4

Reporting Historical Research

p. 13

1. A (interesting opener)
2. C (overview)
3. B (thesis statement)
4. C (sentence variety)
5. B (main ideas)
6. C (elaboration and details)
7. C (support of thesis)
8. D (summaries)
9. B (sentence variety)
10. C (elaboration and details)
11. D (documentation)
12. B (summary of main points)
13. C (restatement of thesis)
14. A (thought-provoking idea)
15. A (variety of sources)

Answer Key (continued)

Collection 5
Analyzing a Novel

p. 19
1. B (author and title)
2. A (background)
3. D (clear thesis statement)
4. A (introduction of quotation)
5. A (literary evidence)
6. C (explanation of evidence)
7. A (effective organization)
8. B (elaboration)
9. A (elaboration)
10. C (memorable conclusion)

Collection 6
Analyzing and Using Media

p. 22
1. D (clear thesis)
2. A (key point)
3. C (visual media support)
4. B (key point)
5. D (visual media support)
6. D (logical order)
7. A (media support)
8. C (key point)
9. D (media support)
10. C (conclusion)

Workshop Scales and Rubrics

NAME _____ CLASS _____ DATE _____

for **COLLECTION 1** page 138

ANALYTICAL SCALE

Writing: Editorial

Use the chart below (and the rubric on pages 34–35) to evaluate an editorial. Circle the numbers that best indicate how well the criteria are met. With eleven criteria, the lowest possible score is 0, the highest 44.

4 = Clearly meets this criterion
3 = Makes a serious effort to meet this criterion and is fairly successful
2 = Makes some effort to meet this criterion but with little success
1 = Does not achieve this criterion
0 = Unscorable

CRITERIA FOR EVALUATION	RATING
Genre, Organization, and Focus	
Introduction grabs the audience's attention.	4 3 2 1
Introduction gives background information.	4 3 2 1
Opinion statement is clear.	4 3 2 1
Reasons and evidence support opinion.	4 3 2 1
Rhetorical devices shape support for opinion.	4 3 2 1
Reasons and evidence are organized on the basis of their relative strength.	4 3 2 1
Conclusion restates opinion.	4 3 2 1
Conclusion gives a call to action.	4 3 2 1
Direct terms replace euphemisms.	4 3 2 1
Language Conventions	
Standard English spelling, punctuation, capitalization, and manuscript form are used appropriately for this grade level.	4 3 2 1
Standard English sentence and paragraph structure, grammar, usage, and diction are used appropriately for this grade level.	4 3 2 1
Total Points:	

Workshop Scales and Rubrics **33**

NAME _____ CLASS _____ DATE _____

for **COLLECTION 1** *page 138*   **ANALYTICAL SCORING RUBRIC**

Writing: Editorial

CRITERIA FOR EVALUATION	SCORE POINT 4	SCORE POINT 3	SCORE POINT 2	SCORE POINT 1
Genre, Organization, and Focus				
Introduction grabs the audience's attention.	Introduction grabs the audience's attention with a question, detail, or anecdote.	Introduction addresses the audience's interests but does not grab their attention.	Introduction only partially addresses the audience's interests.	Introduction is dull or uninteresting.
Introduction gives background information.	Introduction includes solid background information that helps readers understand basic points of the issue.	Introduction includes partial background information that helps readers understand some of the issue's basic points.	Introduction includes very limited background information, which is of little value to readers.	Background information is missing or is irrelevant.
Opinion statement is clear.	Opinion statement clearly states an opinion about a controversial, interesting issue.	Opinion statement identifies an issue, but opinion is unclear.	Opinion statement vaguely identifies an opinion.	Opinion statement cannot be identified or is missing.
Reasons and evidence support opinion.	All reasons and evidence are relevant, support the opinion, and appeal to readers' sense of logic, emotions, or ethical beliefs.	Most reasons and evidence are relevant, support the opinion, and appeal to readers' sense of logic, emotions, or ethical beliefs.	Few reasons or little evidence supports the opinion or appeal to readers' sense of logic, emotions, or ethical beliefs.	Reasons and evidence do not support the opinion or are missing.
Rhetorical devices shape support for opinion.	Rhetorical devices (repetition, parallelism, rhetorical questions, and argument by analogy) persuasively enhance arguments.	Rhetorical devices (repetition, parallelism, rhetorical questions, and argument by analogy) often enhance arguments but not persuasively.	Rhetorical devices are frequently ineffective.	Rhetorical devices are absent.
Reasons and evidence are organized on the basis of their relative strength.	Reasons and evidence are organized for greatest impact on audience and on the basis of their relative strengths.	Reasons and evidence are loosely organized on the basis of their relative strengths.	Organization is unclear or pays little attention to relative strengths of reasons and evidence.	Organization is unclear and confusing.

WORKSHOP SCALES AND RUBRICS

34 Holt Assessment: Writing, Listening, and Speaking

NAME _____ CLASS _____ DATE _____

for COLLECTION 1 continued

ANALYTICAL SCORING RUBRIC

CRITERIA FOR EVALUATION	SCORE POINT 4	SCORE POINT 3	SCORE POINT 2	SCORE POINT 1
Conclusion restates opinion.	Conclusion clearly and freshly restates opinion.	Conclusion clearly but loosely restates opinion.	Conclusion hints at opinion.	Restatement of opinion is missing.
Conclusion gives a call to action.	Conclusion calls readers to action, telling them exactly what to do to change the situation.	Conclusion calls readers to action, imprecisely suggesting what they can do.	Conclusion vaguely hints at what readers might do to change the situation.	Conclusion omits a call to action.
Direct terms replace euphemisms.	Direct, clear terms replace euphemisms.	A few euphemisms appear in the editorial.	Euphemisms are scattered throughout the editorial.	Euphemisms are abundant.
Language Conventions				
Standard English spelling, punctuation, capitalization, and manuscript form are used appropriately for this grade level.	Standard English spelling, punctuation, capitalization, and manuscript form are used appropriately for this grade level throughout the essay.	Standard English spelling, punctuation, capitalization, and manuscript form are used appropriately for this grade level, with few problems.	Inconsistent use of standard English spelling, punctuation, capitalization, and manuscript form sometimes distracts readers.	Minimal use of standard English spelling, punctuation, capitalization, and manuscript form confuses readers.
Standard English sentence and paragraph structure, grammar, usage, and diction are used appropriately for this grade level.	Standard English sentence and paragraph structure, grammar, usage, and diction appropriate for this grade level are used throughout the editorial.	Standard English sentence and paragraph structure, grammar, usage, and diction are used appropriately for this grade level, with a few problems.	Inconsistent use of standard English sentence and paragraph structure, grammar, usage, and diction distracts readers.	Minimal use of standard English sentence and paragraph structure, grammar, usage, and diction confuses readers.

Workshop Scales and Rubrics **35**

NAME _____ CLASS _____ DATE _____

for COLLECTION 1 *page 146*

ANALYTICAL SCALE

Listening and Speaking: Presenting Speeches

Use the chart below to evaluate a persuasive speech. Circle the numbers that best indicate how well the criteria are met. With nine criteria for presenting a speech, the lowest possible score is 0, the highest 36.

4 = Clearly meets this criterion
3 = Makes a serious effort to meet this criterion and is fairly successful
2 = Makes some effort to meet this criterion but with little success
1 = Does not achieve this criterion
0 = Unscorable

CRITERIA FOR EVALUATION	RATING
Content, Organization, and Delivery	
Thought-provoking quotation, touching anecdote, or reference to authority creates dramatic introduction.	4 3 2 1
Strong but simple opinion statement presents distinct perspective on issue.	4 3 2 1
Reasons appeal to the particular audience.	4 3 2 1
Rhetorical devices are effective.	4 3 2 1
Body of speech is organized deductively or inductively.	4 3 2 1
Memorable conclusion summarizes main points and restates opinion directly.	4 3 2 1
Call to action uses specific language.	4 3 2 1
Delivery is polished and well prepared, with careful attention to verbal and nonverbal techniques.	4 3 2 1
Language Conventions	
Standard English grammar, usage, and diction are used appropriately for this grade level.	4 3 2 1
Total Points:	

NAME _____ CLASS _____ DATE _____

for COLLECTION 1 page 146

ANALYTICAL SCALE

Listening and Speaking: Evaluating Speeches

Use the chart below to evaluate students' analysis of a persuasive speech. Circle the numbers that best indicate how well the criteria are met. With three criteria for evaluating a speech, the lowest possible score is 0, the highest 12.

4 = Clearly meets this criterion
3 = Makes a serious effort to meet this criterion and is fairly successful
2 = Makes some effort to meet this criterion but with little success
1 = Does not achieve this criterion
0 = Unscorable

CRITERIA FOR EVALUATION	RATING
THE LISTENER	
Identifies type of persuasive speech (proposition of fact, proposition of policy, proposition of problem, or proposition of value)	4 3 2 1
Evaluates appropriate use of appeals to logic, emotions, or ethics	4 3 2 1
Recognizes use of logical fallacies or propaganda techniques (overgeneralization, false causality, false analogy, red herring, attack *ad hominem*, or bandwagon effect)	4 3 2 1
Total Points:	

Workshop Scales and Rubrics **37**

NAME	CLASS	DATE

for **COLLECTION 2** page 338

ANALYTICAL SCALE

Writing: Short Story

Use the chart below (and the rubric on pages 39–40) to evaluate a short story. Circle the numbers that best indicate how well the criteria are met. With these eleven criteria, the lowest possible score is 0, the highest 44.

4 = Clearly meets this criterion
3 = Makes a serious effort to meet this criterion and is fairly successful
2 = Makes some effort to meet this criterion but with little success
1 = Does not achieve this criterion
0 = Unscorable

CRITERIA FOR EVALUATION	RATING
Genre, Organization, and Focus	
Beginning engages readers' attention.	4 3 2 1
Beginning introduces main characters, gives details about setting, establishes point of view, and sets plot in motion.	4 3 2 1
Characters are developed through specific action, dialogue, interior monologue, description, and concrete sensory details.	4 3 2 1
Point of view is clear and consistently developed.	4 3 2 1
Conflicts introduce plot complications.	4 3 2 1
Plot intensity develops to climax.	4 3 2 1
Ending resolves conflict and reveals final outcome and significance of events.	4 3 2 1
Stylistic devices are used.	4 3 2 1
Precise adjectives help readers visualize characters, setting, and events.	4 3 2 1
Language Conventions	
Standard English spelling, punctuation, capitalization, and manuscript form are used appropriately for this grade level.	4 3 2 1
Standard English sentence and paragraph structure, grammar, usage, and diction are used appropriately for this grade level.	4 3 2 1
Total Points:	

NAME _____ CLASS _____ DATE _____

for **COLLECTION 2** page 338

ANALYTICAL SCORING RUBRIC

Writing: Short Story

CRITERIA FOR EVALUATION	SCORE POINT 4	SCORE POINT 3	SCORE POINT 2	SCORE POINT 1
Genre, Organization, and Focus				
Beginning engages readers' attention.	Beginning engages readers' attention.	Beginning moderately stimulates readers' interest.	Beginning only partially gains readers' attention.	Beginning is trite, dull, or uninteresting.
Beginning introduces main characters, gives details about setting, establishes point of view, and sets plot in motion.	Beginning introduces main characters, gives specific details about setting, firmly establishes point of view, and quickly initiates conflict.	Beginning introduces characters, locates setting, establishes point of view, and initiates conflict.	Beginning names characters and place of setting, hints at point of view, and suggests conflict.	Characters and setting are ignored, point of view is unclear, or initiation of conflict is absent.
Characters are developed through specific action, dialogue, interior monologue, description, and concrete sensory details.	Complex, believable characters are brought to life through specific action, credible dialogue, interior monologue, and descriptive, concrete sensory details.	Somewhat complex characters are created through a general description of behavior, reasonable dialogue or interior monologue, and the use of sensory details.	Characters are presented through vague behaviors, unrealistic dialogue or interior monologue, or the use of few sensory details.	Characters are poorly described and speak or think unrealistically.
Point of view is clear and consistently developed.	Point of view clearly and consistently indicates who tells the story and how much that person knows.	Point of view changes occasionally.	Inconsistent point of view distracts readers.	Abrupt changes in point of view confuse readers.
Conflict introduces plot complications.	Internal or external conflict shown by specific actions, decisions, and events leads to plot complications.	Conflict that characters face sets off a series of plot complications.	Conflict is not clearly developed through plot complications.	Conflict is vague or confusing.
Plot intensity develops to climax.	Intensity of rising action advances the plot toward climax.	Plot leads logically to climax.	Plot loosely leads to climax, or climax occurs at an inappropriate point in story.	Events do not lead to climax, or climax is missing.

WORKSHOP SCALES AND RUBRICS

Workshop Scales and Rubrics **39**

NAME _____ CLASS _____ DATE _____

for **COLLECTION 2** continued

ANALYTICAL SCORING RUBRIC

CRITERIA FOR EVALUATION	SCORE POINT 4	SCORE POINT 3	SCORE POINT 2	SCORE POINT 1
Ending resolves conflict and reveals final outcome and significance of events.	Ending definitely resolves conflict and reveals final outcome and significance of events for the characters in a credible way.	Resolution of conflict and final outcome are clear.	Ending leaves conflict largely unresolved, and final outcome is unclear.	Conflict is not resolved, and final outcome is not mentioned.
Stylistic devices are used.	Consistent use of stylistic devices adds to rhetorical and aesthetic impact of the story.	Use of several stylistic devices makes story more appealing to readers.	Stylistic devices appear only occasionally.	Stylistic devices are missing.
Precise adjectives help readers visualize characters, setting, and events.	Strong, precise adjectives help readers visualize the fictional characters, setting, and dramatic events.	Several precise adjectives help readers visualize characters, setting, and events.	Many vague adjectives detract from the effectiveness of the story.	Most adjectives are vague.
Language Conventions				
Standard English spelling, punctuation, capitalization, and manuscript form are used appropriately for this grade level.	Standard English spelling, punctuation, capitalization, and manuscript form are used appropriately for this grade level throughout the story.	Standard English spelling, punctuation, capitalization, and manuscript form are used appropriately for this grade level, with a few problems.	Inconsistent use of standard English spelling, punctuation, capitalization, and manuscript form distracts readers.	Minimal use of standard English spelling, punctuation, capitalization, and manuscript form confuses readers.
Standard English sentence and paragraph structure, grammar, usage, and diction are used appropriately for this grade level.	Standard English sentence and paragraph structure, grammar, usage, and diction are used appropriately for this grade level.	Standard English sentence and paragraph structure, grammar, usage, and diction are used appropriately for this grade level, with a few problems.	Inconsistent use of standard English sentence and paragraph structure, grammar, usage, and diction distracts readers.	Minimal use of standard English sentence and paragraph structure, grammar, usage, and diction confuses readers.

WORKSHOP SCALES AND RUBRICS

NAME _____ CLASS _____ DATE _____

for **COLLECTION 3** page 426

ANALYTICAL SCALE

Writing: Reflective Essay

Use the chart below (and the rubric on pages 42–43) to evaluate a reflective essay. Circle the numbers that best indicate how well the criteria are met. With these ten criteria, the lowest possible score is 0, the highest 40.

4 = Clearly meets this criterion
3 = Makes a serious effort to meet this criterion and is fairly successful
2 = Makes some effort to meet this criterion but with little success
1 = Does not achieve this criterion
0 = Unscorable

▶ CRITERIA FOR EVALUATION	▶ RATING
Genre, Organization, and Focus	
Introduction captures readers' attention.	4 3 2 1
Introduction provides background information.	4 3 2 1
Introduction hints at significance of experience.	4 3 2 1
Descriptive and narrative details describe people, places, and events.	4 3 2 1
Order of events is clear and makes sense.	4 3 2 1
Conclusion makes significance of experience clear.	4 3 2 1
Conclusion makes connection between the experience and life in general.	4 3 2 1
Colloquial expressions replace overly formal words and phrases.	4 3 2 1
Language Conventions	
Standard English spelling, punctuation, capitalization, and manuscript form are used appropriately for this grade level.	4 3 2 1
Standard English sentence and paragraph structure, grammar, usage, and diction are used appropriately for this grade level.	4 3 2 1
Total Points:	

WORKSHOP SCALES AND RUBRICS

Workshop Scales and Rubrics

NAME _____ CLASS _____ DATE _____

for **COLLECTION 3** page 426

ANALYTICAL SCORING RUBRIC

Writing: Reflective Essay

CRITERIA FOR EVALUATION	SCORE POINT 4	SCORE POINT 3	SCORE POINT 2	SCORE POINT 1
Genre, Organization, and Focus				
Introduction captures readers' attention.	Introduction engages readers' attention with an anecdote, question, or interesting statement.	Introduction takes readers' interests into account.	Introduction only partially gains readers' attention.	Introduction is dull and uninteresting.
Introduction provides background information.	Introduction provides readers with background information that establishes specific context for the experience.	Introduction provides readers with general context for the experience.	Introduction provides little background information.	Background information is missing.
Introduction hints at significance of experience.	Introduction hints at significance of experience, conveying the larger meaning to readers.	Introduction explicitly states significance of experience instead of hinting at it.	Significance of experience is difficult to discern.	Significance of experience is absent in the introduction.
Descriptive and narrative details describe people, places, and events.	Ample descriptive and narrative details that describe people, places, and events bring the experience to life and convince readers of its significance.	Descriptive and narrative details describe a fairly complete picture of people, places, and events.	Descriptions of people, places, and events are general or sparse.	Descriptive and narrative details are missing from the essay.
Order of events is clear and makes sense.	Events are presented in a clear, logical order that makes sense to readers.	Order of events is generally clear and makes sense.	Order makes connections between events difficult to determine.	Order of events is confusing.
Conclusion makes significance of experience clear.	Conclusion includes an explicit statement of the experience's significance.	Conclusion includes a general suggestion of the experience's significance.	Conclusion vaguely hints at the significance of the experience.	Conclusion omits the significance of the experience.

WORKSHOP SCALES AND RUBRICS

42 Holt Assessment: Writing, Listening, and Speaking

for **COLLECTION 3** continued

ANALYTICAL SCORING RUBRIC

CRITERIA FOR EVALUATION	SCORE POINT 4	SCORE POINT 3	SCORE POINT 2	SCORE POINT 1
Conclusion makes connection between the experience and life in general.	Final statement directly connects the specific experience to life in general.	Conclusion makes a loose connection between the experience and life in general.	Essay ends with a statement about life in general that is unconnected to the specific experience.	A statement about life in general is missing from conclusion.
Colloquial expressions replace overly formal words and phrases.	Natural, informal language and effective use of colloquial expressions create a consistently conversational voice.	Fairly natural language and occasional use of colloquial expressions create a generally conversational voice.	Frequent use of overly formal language creates a distracting, unnatural, and stuffy voice.	Reliance on overly formal language hides the writer's voice.

Language Conventions

Standard English spelling, punctuation, capitalization, and manuscript form are used appropriately for this grade level.	Standard English spelling, punctuation, capitalization, and manuscript form are used appropriately for this grade level throughout the reflective essay.	Standard English spelling, punctuation, capitalization, and manuscript form are used appropriately for this grade level, with a few problems.	Inconsistent use of standard English spelling, punctuation, capitalization, and manuscript form distracts readers.	Minimal use of standard English spelling, punctuation, capitalization, and manuscript form confuses readers.
Standard English sentence and paragraph structure, grammar, usage, and diction are used appropriately for this grade level.	Standard English sentence and paragraph structure, grammar, usage, and diction appropriate for this grade level are used throughout the reflective essay.	Standard English sentence and paragraph structure, grammar, usage, and diction appropriate for this grade level are used, with a few problems.	Inconsistent use of standard English sentence and paragraph structure, grammar, usage, and diction distracts readers.	Minimal use of standard English sentence and paragraph structure, grammar, usage, and diction confuses readers.

Workshop Scales and Rubrics

NAME _____ CLASS _____ DATE _____

for **COLLECTION 3** page 434

ANALYTICAL SCALE

Speaking: Presenting a Reflection

Use the chart below to evaluate a reflective presentation. Circle the numbers that best indicate how well the criteria are met. With these seven criteria, the lowest possible score is 0, the highest 28.

4 = Clearly meets this criterion
3 = Makes a serious effort to meet this criterion and is fairly successful
2 = Makes some effort to meet this criterion but with little success
1 = Does not achieve this criterion
0 = Unscorable

CRITERIA FOR EVALUATION	RATING
Content, Organization, and Delivery	
Presentation strikes a balance between showing events and expressing their meaning.	4 3 2 1
Where appropriate, actions or appearances are shown through dialogue or sound and visual effects.	4 3 2 1
Presentation relies on clear, forceful, interesting language.	4 3 2 1
Presentation is delivered extemporaneously using note cards.	4 3 2 1
Verbal techniques (language, tone, and volume) are appropriate to purpose of presentation.	4 3 2 1
Effective use of nonverbal techniques (eye contact, gestures, and facial expressions) engages the audience.	4 3 2 1
Language Conventions	
Standard English grammar, usage, and diction are used appropriately for this grade level.	4 3 2 1
Total Points:	

WORKSHOP SCALES AND RUBRICS

44   Holt Assessment: Writing, Listening, and Speaking

NAME _____ CLASS _____ DATE _____

for **COLLECTION 4** page 602 — **ANALYTICAL SCALE**

Writing: Reporting Historical Research

Use the chart below (and the rubric on pages 46–48) to evaluate a historical research paper. Circle the numbers that best indicate how well the criteria are met. With twelve criteria, the lowest possible score is 0, the highest 48.

4 = Clearly meets this criterion
3 = Makes a serious effort to meet this criterion and is fairly successful
2 = Makes some effort to meet this criterion but with little success
1 = Does not achieve this criterion
0 = Unscorable

CRITERIA FOR EVALUATION	RATING
Genre, Organization, and Delivery	
Introduction draws readers into the research with an interesting opener.	4 3 2 1
Introduction gives an overview of the research and states the thesis.	4 3 2 1
Several main ideas develop the thesis.	4 3 2 1
Facts and details from a variety of primary and secondary sources support the main ideas.	4 3 2 1
Ideas are in logical order.	4 3 2 1
Paper includes summaries, paraphrases, and direct quotations.	4 3 2 1
Conclusion restates the thesis and summarizes the main points.	4 3 2 1
A concluding thought or thought-provoking idea brings the paper to a close.	4 3 2 1
Sources are cited in correct MLA format.	4 3 2 1
Sentence beginnings are varied.	4 3 2 1
Language Conventions	
Standard English spelling, punctuation, capitalization, and manuscript form are used appropriately for this grade level.	4 3 2 1
Standard English sentence and paragraph structure, grammar, usage, and diction are used appropriately for this grade level.	4 3 2 1
Total Points:	

NAME _____ CLASS _____ DATE _____

for **COLLECTION 4** page 602   ANALYTICAL SCORING RUBRIC

Writing: Reporting Historical Research

CRITERIA FOR EVALUATION	SCORE POINT 4	SCORE POINT 3	SCORE POINT 2	SCORE POINT 1
Genre, Organization, and Focus				
Introduction draws readers into the research with an interesting opener.	Introduction quickly draws readers into the research with a quotation or interesting detail.	Introduction draws some readers into the research with relevant opener.	Introduction merely states the topic without accounting for readers' interest.	Introduction is dull or missing.
Introduction gives an overview of the research and states the thesis.	Introduction gives a concise overview of the research and states the topic and a general conclusion.	Introduction gives an overview of the research and states an imprecise thesis.	Introduction gives a sketchy overview of the research, and the thesis merely names the topic.	Introduction lacks an overview of the research and the thesis.
Several main ideas develop the thesis.	Several clearly elaborated main ideas develop the thesis.	Main ideas develop the thesis, but another main idea is needed, or one main idea is unrelated to the thesis.	Few main ideas develop the thesis, more main ideas are necessary, or several are unrelated to the thesis.	Main ideas are unrelated to the thesis, or they are impossible to determine.
Facts and details from a variety of primary and secondary sources support the main ideas.	Facts and details from a variety and balance of reliable primary and secondary sources cover all relevant perspectives and support the main ideas.	Facts and details from variety of both primary and secondary sources support the main ideas, although sources are not balanced.	Facts and details from either primary or secondary sources support some main ideas.	Facts and details are from a single source, no source is apparent, or facts and details do not support main ideas.
Ideas are in logical order.	Ideas are in logical order throughout the paper; there may be a combination of chronological order, logical order, and order of importance, based on the ideas within each section.	Most ideas are in logical order, although some ideas do not flow in a logical progression.	Some ideas are in logical order.	Order of ideas is random.

WORKSHOP SCALES AND RUBRICS

46   Holt Assessment: Writing, Listening, and Speaking

NAME _____ CLASS _____ DATE _____

for COLLECTION 4 *continued*   **ANALYTICAL SCORING RUBRIC**

CRITERIA FOR EVALUATION	SCORE POINT 4	SCORE POINT 3	SCORE POINT 2	SCORE POINT 1
Paper includes summaries, paraphrases, and direct quotations.	Paper effectively and appropriately includes a balance of summaries, paraphrases, and direct quotations.	Paper includes summaries, paraphrases, and direct quotations, although they are not always used suitably.	Paper includes summaries, paraphrases, and direct quotations, but it mostly has a single type of information.	Paper is largely composed of direct quotations, or it is impossible to determine what is directly quoted.
Conclusion restates the thesis and summarizes the main points.	Conclusion clearly and freshly restates the thesis and succinctly summarizes the main points.	Conclusion restates the thesis and summarizes some main points.	Conclusion exactly restates or only hints at thesis and does not summarize main points.	Conclusion is missing, and paper ends abruptly.
A concluding thought or thought-provoking idea brings the paper to a close.	A well-supported concluding thought or thought-provoking idea brings the paper to a close.	A concluding thought or thought-provoking idea brings the paper to a close, although the thought is not directly based on the information in the report.	A concluding thought or idea is not based on information in the paper.	Paper has no apparent close.
Sources are cited in correct MLA format.	Sources are clearly and correctly cited and included in a *Works Cited* list.	Sources are correctly cited and included in a *Works Cited* list, with few errors or omissions.	A few sources are correctly cited, but most citations are incomplete or incorrect.	Neither textual citations nor a *Works Cited* list is included.
Sentence beginnings are varied.	Interesting use of adverb clauses results in fresh, refined sentence beginnings.	Use of adverb clauses for sentence beginnings adds variety.	An occasional use of adverb clauses improves some sentence beginnings.	Most sentences begin the same way.
▶ **Language Conventions**				
Standard English spelling, punctuation, capitalization, and manuscript form are used appropriately for this grade level.	Standard English spelling, punctuation, capitalization, and manuscript form are used appropriately for this grade level throughout the paper.	Standard English spelling, punctuation, capitalization, and manuscript form are used appropriately for this grade level, with a few problems.	Inconsistent use of standard English spelling, punctuation, capitalization, and manuscript form distracts readers.	Minimal use of standard English spelling, punctuation, capitalization, and manuscript form confuses readers.

WORKSHOP SCALES AND RUBRICS

Workshop Scales and Rubrics   **47**

NAME _____ CLASS _____ DATE _____

for COLLECTION 4 continued

ANALYTICAL SCORING RUBRIC

CRITERIA FOR EVALUATION	SCORE POINT 4	SCORE POINT 3	SCORE POINT 2	SCORE POINT 1
Standard English sentence and paragraph structure, grammar, usage, and diction are used appropriately for this grade level.	Standard English sentence and paragraph structure, grammar, usage, and diction are used appropriately for this grade level throughout the paper.	Standard English sentence and paragraph structure, grammar, usage, and diction are used appropriately for this grade level, with a few problems.	Inconsistent use of standard English sentence and paragraph structure, grammar, usage, and diction distracts readers.	Minimal use of standard English sentence and paragraph structure, grammar, usage, and diction confuses readers.

NAME _____ CLASS _____ DATE _____

for **COLLECTION 4** page 622

ANALYTICAL SCALE

Speaking: Presenting Historical Research

Use the chart below to evaluate an oral report of historical research. Circle the numbers that best indicate how well the criteria are met. With these nine criteria, the lowest possible score is 0, the highest 36.

4 = Clearly meets this criterion
3 = Makes a serious effort to meet this criterion and is fairly successful
2 = Makes some effort to meet this criterion but with little success
1 = Does not achieve this criterion
0 = Unscorable

CRITERIA FOR EVALUATION	RATING
Content, Organization, and Delivery	
Introduction gives background information.	4 3 2 1
Thesis clearly communicates conclusions about the topic.	4 3 2 1
A balance of primary and secondary sources represents relevant perspectives on topic.	4 3 2 1
A combination of rhetorical strategies (exposition, narration, description, and persuasion) presents findings in clear, concise, and interesting way.	4 3 2 1
Authors and sources are named.	4 3 2 1
Summary of main ideas and restatement of thesis in conclusion are obvious and simply presented.	4 3 2 1
Verbal techniques (tone, volume, pauses, and rate) help the audience focus on presentation.	4 3 2 1
Nonverbal techniques (eye contact, facial expressions, gestures, and posture) contribute to the quality of the presentation.	4 3 2 1
Language Conventions	
Standard English grammar, usage, and diction are used appropriately for this grade level.	4 3 2 1
Total Points:	

NAME _____ CLASS _____ DATE _____

for **COLLECTION 5** page 679

ANALYTICAL SCALE

Writing: Descriptive Essay

Use the chart below to evaluate a descriptive essay. Circle the numbers that best indicate how well the criteria are met. With these five criteria, the lowest possible score is 0, the highest 20.

4 = Clearly meets this criterion
3 = Makes a serious effort to meet this criterion and is fairly successful
2 = Makes some effort to meet this criterion but with little success
1 = Does not achieve this criterion
0 = Unscorable

CRITERIA FOR EVALUATION	RATING
Genre, Organization, and Focus	
Statement of controlling impression prepares audience for writer's ideas.	4 3 2 1
Essential details (concrete sensory details, action details, and details about changes) contribute to the controlling impression, set the tone for the essay, and help readers visualize the subject.	4 3 2 1
Language is fresh and natural.	4 3 2 1
Ideas are organized effectively, using either spatial order or order of importance.	4 3 2 1
Language Conventions	
Standard English-language conventions are used appropriately for this grade level.	4 3 2 1
Total Points:	

WORKSHOP SCALES AND RUBRICS

50 Holt Assessment: Writing, Listening, and Speaking

NAME _____ CLASS _____ DATE _____

for **COLLECTION 5** page 739

ANALYTICAL SCALE

Writing: Analyzing Literature

Use the chart below to evaluate a short story analysis. Circle the numbers that best indicate how well the criteria are met. With these four criteria, the lowest possible score is 0, the highest 16.

4 = Clearly meets this criterion
3 = Makes a serious effort to meet this criterion and is fairly successful
2 = Makes some effort to meet this criterion but with little success
1 = Does not achieve this criterion
0 = Unscorable

CRITERIA FOR EVALUATION	RATING
Genre, Organization, and Focus	
Thesis statement identifies the point to be made about a specific literary element.	4 3 2 1
Accurate and detailed literary evidence from the short story and/or secondary sources supports thesis statement.	4 3 2 1
Essay is organized by order of importance or chronological order.	4 3 2 1
Language Conventions	
Standard English-language conventions are used appropriately for this grade level.	4 3 2 1
Total Points:	

NAME _____ CLASS _____ DATE _____

for **COLLECTION 5** *page 813*

ANALYTICAL SCALE

Writing: Biographical Narrative

Use the chart below to evaluate a biographical narrative. Circle the numbers that best indicate how well the criteria are met. With these nine criteria, the lowest possible score is 0, the highest 36.

4 = Clearly meets this criterion
3 = Makes a serious effort to meet this criterion and is fairly successful
2 = Makes some effort to meet this criterion but with little success
1 = Does not achieve this criterion
0 = Unscorable

▶ CRITERIA FOR EVALUATION	▶ RATING
▶ **Genre, Organization, and Focus**	
Narrative focuses on an incident in the life of the person.	4 3 2 1
Narrative and descriptive details bring the subject and the incident to life.	4 3 2 1
Concrete sensory details create specific images in readers' minds.	4 3 2 1
Interior monologue allows readers to experience the subject's thoughts.	4 3 2 1
Point of view is consistent, or if perspective shifts, transitions are clear.	4 3 2 1
In general, the narrative is presented in chronological order.	4 3 2 1
Pace varies to accommodate spatial, temporal, and dramatic mood changes.	4 3 2 1
Direct statement about the subject's character ends the narrative.	4 3 2 1
▶ **Language Conventions**	
Standard English-language conventions are used appropriately for this grade level.	4 3 2 1
Total Points:	

NAME _____ CLASS _____ DATE _____

for COLLECTION 5 *page 870*

ANALYTICAL SCALE

Writing: Analyzing a Novel

Use the chart below (and the rubric on pages 54–55) to evaluate an analysis of a novel. Circle the numbers that best indicate how well the criteria are met. With these nine criteria, the lowest possible score is 0, the highest 36.

4 = Clearly meets this criterion
3 = Makes a serious effort to meet this criterion and is fairly successful
2 = Makes some effort to meet this criterion but with little success
1 = Does not achieve this criterion
0 = Unscorable

CRITERIA FOR EVALUATION	RATING
Genre, Organization, and Focus	
Introduction presents background information, author's name, and novel's title.	4 3 2 1
Introduction includes clear thesis statement.	4 3 2 1
Major points are organized in a logical order.	4 3 2 1
Literary evidence supports each major point.	4 3 2 1
Elaboration explains how evidence supports major points.	4 3 2 1
Conclusion restates thesis and summarizes major points.	4 3 2 1
Analysis ends with memorable statement.	4 3 2 1
Language Conventions	
Standard English spelling, punctuation, capitalization, and manuscript form are used appropriately for this grade level.	4 3 2 1
Standard English sentence and paragraph structure, grammar, usage, and diction are used appropriately for this grade level.	4 3 2 1
Total Points:	

Workshop Scales and Rubrics

NAME _____ CLASS _____ DATE _____

for **COLLECTION 5** page 870

ANALYTICAL SCORING RUBRIC

Writing: Analyzing a Novel

CRITERIA FOR EVALUATION	SCORE POINT 4	SCORE POINT 3	SCORE POINT 2	SCORE POINT 1
Genre, Organization, and Focus				
Introduction presents background information, author's name, and novel's title.	Introduction presents author's name, novel's title, and pertinent, essential background information to provide context for the analysis.	Introduction presents author's name, novel's title, and sufficient background information to provide context for the analysis.	Introduction presents author's name or novel's title but offers little or no useful background information.	Introduction provides no background information and does not give author's name or novel's title.
Introduction includes clear thesis statement.	Thesis statement presents a clear conclusion about the literary element on which the analysis focuses.	Thesis statement identifies the literary element and presents the writer's conclusion fairly clearly.	Thesis statement vaguely identifies the literary element but does not present the writer's conclusion.	Introduction includes no thesis statement.
Major points are organized in a logical order.	Major points are clearly organized by chronological order or order of importance, with each body paragraph developing a major point.	Most major points are organized by chronological order or order of importance.	Several major points are out of order.	Major points are presented in no particular order.
Literary evidence supports each major point.	Quotations, paraphrases, and summaries from text and evidence from secondary sources support major points.	Details from text and some evidence from secondary sources support most major points.	A few details from text or secondary sources support some major points.	Details from text or secondary sources are missing or do not support major points.
Elaboration explains how evidence supports major points.	Elaboration on importance of each idea, ambiguities, nuances, and complexities plainly supports and connects points to thesis.	Elaboration on main points, ambiguities, nuances, and complexities supports major points but does not explain connection to the thesis.	Elaboration is sparse.	Essay does not elaborate on how evidence supports major points.

WORKSHOP SCALES AND RUBRICS

54   Holt Assessment: Writing, Listening, and Speaking

NAME _____ CLASS _____ DATE _____

for COLLECTION 5 *continued*   ANALYTICAL SCORING RUBRIC

CRITERIA FOR EVALUATION	SCORE POINT 4	SCORE POINT 3	SCORE POINT 2	SCORE POINT 1
Conclusion restates thesis and summarizes major points.	Conclusion freshly restates thesis and summarizes major points.	Conclusion restates thesis and summarizes most major points.	Conclusion exactly restates thesis or summarizes some major points.	Restatement of thesis and summary of major points are missing.
Analysis ends with memorable statement.	Memorable concluding statement presents idea readers can ponder.	Analysis ends with an interesting statement.	Concluding statement is anticlimactic and bland.	Essay contains no concluding statement and ends abruptly.

▶ **Language Conventions**

Standard English spelling, punctuation, capitalization, and manuscript form are used appropriately for this grade level.	Standard English spelling, punctuation, capitalization, and manuscript form are used appropriately for this grade level throughout the essay.	Standard English spelling, punctuation, capitalization, and manuscript form are used appropriately for this grade level, with few problems.	Inconsistent use of standard English, spelling, punctuation, capitalization, and manuscript form distracts readers.	Minimal use of standard English, spelling, punctuation, capitalization, and manuscript form confuses readers.
Standard English sentence and paragraph structure, grammar, usage, and diction are used appropriately for this grade level.	Standard English sentence and paragraph structure, grammar, usage, and diction are used appropriately for this grade level throughout the essay.	Standard English sentence and paragraph structure, grammar, usage, and diction are used appropriately for this grade level, with few problems.	Inconsistent use of standard English sentence and paragraph structure, grammar, usage, and diction distracts readers.	Minimal use of standard English sentence and paragraph structure, grammar, usage, and diction confuses readers.

WORKSHOP SCALES AND RUBRICS

NAME _____ CLASS _____ DATE _____

for **COLLECTION 5** page 878

ANALYTICAL SCALE

Speaking: Presenting a Literary Analysis

Use the chart below to evaluate an oral response to literature. Circle the numbers that best indicate how well the criteria are met. With these six criteria, the lowest possible score is 0, the highest 24.

4 = Clearly meets this criterion
3 = Makes a serious effort to meet this criterion and is fairly successful
2 = Makes some effort to meet this criterion but with little success
1 = Does not achieve this criterion
0 = Unscorable

CRITERIA FOR EVALUATION	RATING
Content, Organization, and Delivery	
Thesis statement shows a comprehensive understanding of significant ideas in the novel.	4 3 2 1
Major points are supported by accurate and detailed references to the text or to secondary sources.	4 3 2 1
Rhetorical techniques (rhetorical questions and parallel structure) help listeners understand and remember the presentation.	4 3 2 1
Presentation follows chronological order or order of importance.	4 3 2 1
Verbal and nonverbal techniques are used effectively.	4 3 2 1
Language Conventions	
Standard English grammar, usage, and diction are used appropriately for this grade level.	4 3 2 1
Total Points:	

56 Holt Assessment: Writing, Listening, and Speaking

NAME _____ CLASS _____ DATE _____

for COLLECTION 5 page 1060

ANALYTICAL SCALE

Writing: Autobiographical Narrative

Use the chart below to evaluate an autobiographical narrative. Circle the numbers that best indicate how well the criteria are met. With these six criteria, the lowest possible score is 0, the highest 24.

4 = Clearly meets this criterion
3 = Makes a serious effort to meet this criterion and is fairly successful
2 = Makes some effort to meet this criterion but with little success
1 = Does not achieve this criterion
0 = Unscorable

CRITERIA FOR EVALUATION	RATING
Genre, Organization, and Focus	
Introduction hints at meaning of experience.	4 3 2 1
Background information provides a context for the events.	4 3 2 1
Main events are narrated in order appropriate to story.	4 3 2 1
Narrative and descriptive details flesh out sequence of events and make experience vivid for readers.	4 3 2 1
Conclusion includes direct statement of experience's significance or explains its importance.	4 3 2 1
Language Conventions	
Standard English-language conventions are used appropriately for this grade level.	4 3 2 1
Total Points:	

NAME _____ CLASS _____ DATE _____

for COLLECTION 6 page 1127

ANALYTICAL SCALE

Writing: Analyzing Nonfiction

Use the chart below to evaluate an analysis of nonfiction. Circle the numbers that best indicate how well the criteria are met. With these five criteria, the lowest possible score is 0, the highest 20.

4 = Clearly meets this criterion
3 = Makes a serious effort to meet this criterion and is fairly successful
2 = Makes some effort to meet this criterion but with little success
1 = Does not achieve this criterion
0 = Unscorable

CRITERIA FOR EVALUATION	RATING
Genre, Organization, and Focus	
Thesis statement identifies literary elements to be analyzed and expresses main idea about them.	4 3 2 1
Essay analyzes the literary elements used to achieve specific rhetorical and aesthetic goals.	4 3 2 1
Precise and relevant examples from text (direct quotations, paraphrases, and summaries) support ideas.	4 3 2 1
Organizational pattern, either chronological order or order of importance, is clear and logical.	4 3 2 1
Language Conventions	
Standard English-language conventions are used appropriately for this grade level.	4 3 2 1
Total Points:	

NAME _____ CLASS _____ DATE _____

for COLLECTION 6 *page 1314*

ANALYTICAL SCALE

Media: Analyzing Media

Use the chart below to evaluate an analysis of a media presentation. Circle the numbers that best indicate how well the criteria are met. With these five criteria, the lowest possible score is 0, the highest 20.

4 = Clearly meets this criterion
3 = Makes a serious effort to meet this criterion and is fairly successful
2 = Makes some effort to meet this criterion but with little success
1 = Does not achieve this criterion
0 = Unscorable

CRITERIA FOR EVALUATION	RATING
Genre, Organization, and Focus	
Purpose or purposes of media messages are identified.	4 3 2 1
Media literacy concepts are used to analyze, interpret, and evaluate messages.	4 3 2 1
Media strategies (language, stereotypes, special effects, and visual representations) are identified, and effectiveness of strategies is interpreted and evaluated.	4 3 2 1
If applicable, messages are decoded and analyzed for impact on democratic process.	4 3 2 1
Language Conventions	
Standard English-language conventions are used appropriately for this grade level.	4 3 2 1
Total Points:	

Workshop Scales and Rubrics

NAME _____ CLASS _____ DATE _____

for **COLLECTION 6** page 1314

ANALYTICAL SCALE

Media: Using Media

Use the chart below to evaluate a multimedia presentation. Circle the numbers that best indicate how well the criteria are met. With these seven criteria, the lowest possible score is 0, the highest 28.

4 = Clearly meets this criterion
3 = Makes a serious effort to meet this criterion and is fairly successful
2 = Makes some effort to meet this criterion but with little success
1 = Does not achieve this criterion
0 = Unscorable

CRITERIA FOR EVALUATION	RATING
Content, Organization, and Focus	
Clear thesis statement encompasses key points and states the focus of the presentation.	4 3 2 1
Text, images, and sound from a variety of media sources elaborate on presentation's content and add to the aesthetic appeal and effectiveness.	4 3 2 1
Support chosen is appropriate for each part of the presentation.	4 3 2 1
Media used is of high quality and is incorporated judiciously into the presentation.	4 3 2 1
Presentation is organized by order of importance, with the use of note cards and outline.	4 3 2 1
Presentation is well rehearsed and smooth; delivery is clear and natural.	4 3 2 1
Language Conventions	
Standard English grammar, usage, and diction are used appropriately for this grade level.	4 3 2 1
Total Points:	

NAME _____ CLASS _____ DATE _____

for COLLECTION 6 *page 1322*

ANALYTICAL SCALE

Speaking: Reciting Literature

Use the chart below to evaluate a recitation of a literary work. Circle the numbers that best indicate how well the criteria are met. With these six criteria, the lowest possible score is 0, the highest 24.

4 = Clearly meets this criterion
3 = Makes a serious effort to meet this criterion and is fairly successful
2 = Makes some effort to meet this criterion but with little success
1 = Does not achieve this criterion
0 = Unscorable

CRITERIA FOR EVALUATION	RATING
Choice and Delivery	
Brief introduction catches listeners' interest, includes title of selection and author's name, and provides background information.	4 3 2 1
Selection is relevant and suitable to audience.	4 3 2 1
Performance details (pronunciation, enunciation, characterizations, and dialect, when appropriate) make the presentation clear, forceful, and aesthetically pleasing.	4 3 2 1
Interpretive techniques and nonverbal language are used effectively in recitation.	4 3 2 1
Selection is recited from memory.	4 3 2 1
Language Conventions	
In the introduction, standard English grammar, usage, and diction are used appropriately for this grade level.	4 3 2 1
Total Points:	

WORKSHOP SCALES AND RUBRICS

Workshop Scales and Rubrics **61**

Scales and Sample Papers

Analytical Scale: 7 Writing Traits

IDEAS AND CONTENT

Score 5

The paper is clear, focused, and engaging. Its thoughtful, concrete details capture the reader's attention and flesh out the central theme, main idea, or story line.

- A score "5" paper has the following characteristics.
  - ✓ The topic is clearly focused and manageable for a paper of its kind; it is not overly broad or scattered.
  - ✓ Ideas are original and creative.
  - ✓ The writer appears to be working from personal knowledge or experience.
  - ✓ Key details are insightful and well considered; they are not obvious, predictable, or humdrum.
  - ✓ The development of the topic is thorough and purposeful; the writer anticipates and answers the reader's questions.
  - ✓ Supporting details are never superfluous or merely ornamental; every detail contributes to the whole.

Score 3

The writer develops the topic in a general or basic way; although clear, the paper remains routine or broad.

- A score "3" paper has the following characteristics.
  - ✓ Although the topic may be fuzzy, it is still possible to understand the writer's purpose and to predict how the paper will be developed.
  - ✓ Support is present, but somewhat vague and unhelpful in illustrating the key issues or main idea; the writer makes references to his or her own experience or knowledge, but has difficulty moving from general observations to specifics.
  - ✓ Ideas are understandable, yet not detailed, elaborated upon, or personalized; the writer's ideas do not reveal any deep comprehension of the topic or of the writing task.
  - ✓ The writer does not stray from the topic, but ideas remain general or slightly implicit; more information is necessary to fill in the gaps.

Score 1

The paper does not exhibit any clear purpose or main idea. The reader must use the scattered details to infer a coherent and meaningful message.

- A score "1" paper has the following characteristics.
  - ✓ The writer seems not to have truly settled on a topic; the essay reads like a series of brainstorming notes or disconnected, random thoughts.
  - ✓ The thesis is a vague statement of the topic rather than a main idea about the topic; in addition, there is little or no support or detail.
  - ✓ Information is very limited or vague; readers must make inferences to fill in gaps of logic or to identify any progression of ideas.
  - ✓ Text may be rambling and repetitious; alternatively, the length may not be adequate for a thoughtful development of ideas.
  - ✓ There is no subordination of ideas; every idea seems equally weighted or ideas are not tied to an overarching idea.

Analytical Scale: 7 Writing Traits (continued)

ORGANIZATION

Score 5

Organization enables the clear communication of the central idea or story line. The order of information draws the reader effortlessly through the text.

- *A score "5" paper has the following characteristics.*
  - ✓ The sequencing is logical and effective; ideas and details "fit" where the writer has placed them.
  - ✓ The essay contains an interesting or inviting introduction and a satisfying conclusion.
  - ✓ The pacing is carefully controlled; the writer slows down to provide explanation or elaboration when appropriate and increases the pace when necessary.
  - ✓ Transitions carefully connect ideas and cue the reader to specific relationships between ideas.
  - ✓ The choice of organizational structure is appropriate to the writer's purpose and audience.
  - ✓ If present, the title sums up the central idea of the paper in a fresh or thoughtful way.

Score 3

Organization is reasonably strong; it enables the reader to move continually forward without undue confusion.

- *A score "3" paper has the following characteristics.*
  - ✓ The essay has an introduction and conclusion. However, the introduction may not be inviting or engaging; the conclusion may not knit all the paper's ideas together with a summary or restatement.
  - ✓ Sequencing is logical but predictable. Sometimes, the sequence may be so formulaic that it detracts from the content.
  - ✓ At times, the sequence may not consistently support the essay's ideas; the reader may wish to reorder sections mentally or to supply transitions as he or she reads.
  - ✓ Pacing is reasonably well done, although sometimes the writer moves ahead too quickly or spends too much time on unimportant details.
  - ✓ At times, transitions may be fuzzy, showing unclear connections between ideas.
  - ✓ If present, the title may be dull or a simple restatement of the topic or prompt.

Score 1

Writing does not exhibit a sense of purpose or writing strategy. Ideas, details, or events appear to be cobbled together without any internal structure.

- *A score "1" paper has the following characteristics.*
  - ✓ Sequencing needs work; one idea or event does not logically follow another. Organizational problems make it difficult for the reader to understand the main idea.
  - ✓ There is no real introduction to guide the reader into the paper; neither is there any real conclusion or attempt to tie things up at the end.
  - ✓ Pacing is halting or inconsistent; the writer may slow the pace or speed up at inappropriate times.
  - ✓ Ideas are connected with confusing transitions; alternatively, connections are altogether absent.
  - ✓ If present, the title does not accurately reflect the content of the essay.

Analytical Scale: 7 Writing Traits (continued)

VOICE

Score 5

The writing is expressive and engaging. In addition, the writer seems to have a clear awareness of audience and purpose.

- *A score "5" paper has the following characteristics.*
  - ✓ The tone of the writing is appropriate for the purpose and audience of the paper.
  - ✓ The reader is aware of a real person behind the text; if appropriate, the writer takes risks in revealing a personal dimension throughout the piece.
  - ✓ If the paper is expository or persuasive, the writer shows a strong connection to the topic and explains why the reader should care about the issue.
  - ✓ If the paper is a narrative, the point of view is sincere, interesting, and compelling.

Score 3

The writer is reasonably genuine but does not reveal any excitement or connection with the issue. The resulting paper is pleasant but not truly engaging.

- *A score "3" paper has the following characteristics.*
  - ✓ The writer offers obvious generalities instead of personal insights.
  - ✓ The writer uses neutral language and a slightly flattened tone.
  - ✓ The writer communicates in an earnest and pleasing manner, yet takes no risks. In only a few instances is the reader captivated or moved.
  - ✓ Expository or persuasive writing does not reveal a consistent engagement with the topic; there is no attempt to build credibility with the audience.
  - ✓ Narrative writing doesn't reveal a fresh or individual perspective.

Score 1

Writing is mechanical or wooden. The writer appears indifferent to the topic and/or the audience.

- *A score "1" paper has the following characteristics.*
  - ✓ The writer shows no concern with the audience, the voice may be jarringly inappropriate for the intended reader.
  - ✓ The development of the topic is so limited that no identifiable point of view is present, or the writing is so short that it offers little but a general introduction of the topic.
  - ✓ The writer seems to speak in a monotone, using a voice that suppresses all excitement about the message.
  - ✓ Although the writing may communicate on a functional level, the writing is ordinary and takes no risks; depending on the topic, it may be overly technical or jargonistic.

Scales and Sample Papers

Analytical Scale: 7 Writing Traits (continued)

WORD CHOICE

Score 5

Words are precise, engaging, and unaffected. They convey the writer's message in an interesting and effective way.

- *A score "5" paper has the following characteristics.*
  - ✓ All words are specific and appropriate. In all instances, the writer has taken care to choose the right words or phrases.
  - ✓ The paper's language is natural, not overwrought; it never shows a lack of control. Clichés and jargon are rarely used.
  - ✓ The paper contains energetic verbs; precise nouns and modifiers provide clarity.
  - ✓ The writer uses vivid words and phrases, including sensory details; such language creates distinct images in the reader's mind.

Score 3

Despite its lack of flair, the paper's language gets the message across. It is functional and clear.

- *A score "3" paper has the following characteristics.*
  - ✓ Words are correct and generally adequate, but lack originality or precision.
  - ✓ Familiar words and phrases do not pique the reader's interest or imagination. Lively verbs and phrases perk things up occasionally, but the paper does not consistently sparkle.
  - ✓ There are attempts at engaging or academic language, but they sometimes seem overly showy or pretentious.
  - ✓ The writing contains passive verbs and basic nouns and adjectives, and it lacks precise adverbs.

Score 1

The writer's limited vocabulary impedes communication; he or she seems to struggle for words to convey a clear message.

- *A score "1" paper has the following characteristics.*
  - ✓ Vague language communicates an imprecise or incomplete message. The reader is left confused or unsure of the writer's purpose.
  - ✓ Words are used incorrectly. In addition, frequent misuse of parts of speech impairs understanding.
  - ✓ Excessive redundancy in the paper is distracting.
  - ✓ The writing overuses jargon or clichés.

Analytical Scale: 7 Writing Traits *(continued)*

SENTENCE FLUENCY

Score 5

Sentences are thoughtfully constructed, and sentence structure is varied throughout the paper. When read aloud, the writing is fluent and rhythmic.

- *A score "5" paper has the following characteristics.*
  - ✓ The sentences are constructed so that meaning is clear to the reader.
  - ✓ Sentences vary in length and in structure.
  - ✓ Varied sentence beginnings add interest and clarity.
  - ✓ The writing has a steady beat; the reader is able to read the text effortlessly, without confusion or stumbling.
  - ✓ Dialogue, if used, is natural. Any fragments are used purposefully and contribute to the paper's style.
  - ✓ Thoughtful connectives and transitions between sentences reveal how the paper's ideas work together.

Score 3

The text maintains a steady rhythm, but the reader may find it more flat or mechanical than fluent or musical.

- *A score "3" paper has the following characteristics.*
  - ✓ Sentences are usually grammatical and unified, but they are routine rather than artful. The writer has not paid a great deal of attention to how the sentences sound.
  - ✓ There is some variation in sentence length and structure as well as in sentence beginnings. Not all sentences are constructed exactly the same way.
  - ✓ The reader may have to search for transitional words and phrases that show how sentences relate to one another. Sometimes, such context clues are entirely absent when they should be present.
  - ✓ Although sections of the paper invite expressive oral reading, the reader may also encounter many stilted or awkward sections.

Score 1

The reader will encounter challenges in reading the choppy or confusing text; meaning may be significantly obscured by the errors in sentence construction.

- *A score "1" paper has the following characteristics.*
  - ✓ The sentences do not "hang together." They are run-on, incomplete, monotonous, or awkward.
  - ✓ Phrasing often sounds too sing-song, not natural. The paper does not invite expressive oral reading.
  - ✓ Nearly all the sentences begin the same way, and they may all follow the same pattern (e.g., subject-verb-object). The result may be a monotonous repetition of sounds.
  - ✓ Endless connectives or a complete lack of connectives creates a confused muddle of language.

Analytical Scale: 7 Writing Traits *(continued)*

CONVENTIONS

Score 5

Standard writing conventions (e.g., spelling, punctuation, capitalization, grammar, usage, and paragraphing) are used correctly and in a way that aids the reader's understanding. Any errors tend to be minor; the piece is nearly ready for publication.

- *A score "5" paper has the following characteristics.*
  ✓ Paragraphing is regular and enhances the organization of the paper.
  ✓ Grammar and usage are correct and add clarity to the text as a whole. Sometimes, the writer may manipulate conventions in a controlled way—especially grammar and spelling—for stylistic effect.
  ✓ Punctuation is accurate; it enables the reader to move through the text with understanding and ease.
  ✓ The writer's understanding of capitalization rules is evident throughout the paper.
  ✓ Most words, even difficult ones, are spelled correctly.

Score 3

The writer exhibits an awareness of a limited set of standard writing conventions and uses them to enhance the paper's readability. Although the writer shows control, at times errors distract the reader or impede communication. Moderate editing is required for publication.

- *A score "3" paper has the following characteristics.*
  ✓ Paragraphs are used, but may begin in the wrong places, or sections that should be separate paragraphs are run together.
  ✓ Conventions may not always be correct. However, problems with grammar and usage are usually not serious enough to distort meaning.
  ✓ Terminal (end-of-sentence) punctuation is usually correct; internal punctuation (e.g., commas, apostrophes, semicolons, parentheses) may be missing or wrong.
  ✓ Common words are usually spelled correctly.
  ✓ Most words are capitalized correctly, but the writer's command of more sophisticated capitalization skills is inconsistent.

Score 1

There are errors in spelling, punctuation, usage and grammar, capitalization, and/or paragraphing that seriously impede the reader's comprehension. Extensive editing is required for publication.

- *A score "1" paper has the following characteristics.*
  ✓ Paragraphing is missing, uneven, or too frequent. Most of the paragraphs do not reinforce or support the organizational structure of the paper.
  ✓ Errors in grammar and usage are very common and distracting; such errors also affect the paper's meaning.
  ✓ Punctuation, including terminal punctuation, is often missing or incorrect.
  ✓ Even common words are frequently misspelled.
  ✓ Capitalization is haphazard or reveals the writer's understanding of only the simplest rules.
  ✓ The paper must be read once just to decode the language and then again to capture the paper's meaning.

Analytical Scale: 7 Writing Traits *(continued)*

PRESENTATION

Score 5

The presentation of the writing is clear and visually appealing. The format helps the reader focus on the message of the writing.

- *A score "5" paper has the following characteristics.*
  - ✓ If the paper is handwritten, all letters are formed clearly, and the slant and spacing are consistent.
  - ✓ If the paper is word processed, fonts and font sizes are appropriate for the genre of writing and assist the reader's comprehension.
  - ✓ White space and text are balanced.
  - ✓ Text markers, such as title, headings, and numbering, highlight important information and aid reading of the text.
  - ✓ If visuals are used, they are appropriate to the writing, are integrated effectively with the text, and clearly communicate and enhance the message.

Score 3

The presentation of the writing is readable and understandable; however, inconsistencies in format at times detract from the text.

- *A score "3" paper has the following characteristics.*
  - ✓ If the paper is handwritten, the handwriting is legible, but some inconsistencies occur in spacing and the formation and slant of letters.
  - ✓ If the paper is word processed, fonts and font sizes are inconsistent, sometimes distracting the reader.
  - ✓ White space and text are consistent, although a different use of space would make the paper easier to read.
  - ✓ Text markers, such as title, headings, and numbering, are used to some degree; however, they are inconsistent and only occasionally helpful to the reader.
  - ✓ Visuals are sometimes ineffective and not clearly linked to the text.

Score 1

The presentation and format of the writing are confusing, making the paper difficult to read and understand.

- *A score "1" paper has the following characteristics.*
  - ✓ If the paper is handwritten, the letters are formed incorrectly or irregularly. The inconsistent slant and spacing make the paper difficult to read.
  - ✓ If the paper is word processed, fonts and font sizes are used randomly or inappropriately, disrupting the reader's comprehension.
  - ✓ Spacing appears random, with use of white space either excessive or minimal.
  - ✓ Text markers, such as title, headings, and numbering, are not used.
  - ✓ Visuals are inaccurate, inappropriate, misleading, or confusing.

Biographical or Autobiographical Narrative Holistic Scale

Score 4

This distinctly purposeful narrative has an engaging and meaningful introduction, presents a logical sequence of events, and relies on concrete sensory details. The significance of the events is clearly communicated.

- *The writing strongly demonstrates*
  - ✓ thorough attention to all parts of the writing task
  - ✓ a strong and meaningful purpose, consistent tone and focus, and thoughtfully effective organization
  - ✓ a distinct understanding of audience
  - ✓ great proficiency in relating a sequence of events and their significance to the audience
  - ✓ consistent use of concrete sensory details to describe the sights, sounds, and smells of a scene
  - ✓ variation of sentence types using precise, descriptive language
  - ✓ a solid command of English-language conventions. Errors, if any, are minor and unobtrusive.

Score 3

This purposeful narrative has a meaningful introduction, presents a logical sequence of events, and clearly communicates the significance of those events.

- *The writing generally demonstrates*
  - ✓ attention to all parts of the writing task
  - ✓ clear purpose, a consistent tone and focus, and effective organization
  - ✓ an understanding of audience
  - ✓ an ability to relate a sequence of events and their significance to the audience
  - ✓ frequent use of concrete sensory details to describe the sights, sounds, and smells of a scene
  - ✓ variation of sentence types using some descriptive language
  - ✓ a command of English-language conventions. Few errors exist, and they do not interfere with the reader's understanding of the narrative.

Score 2

This narrative has a somewhat vague introduction. The sequence or significance of the events is unclear.

- *The writing demonstrates*
  - ✓ attention to only parts of the writing task
  - ✓ vague purpose, an inconsistent tone and focus, and less than effective organization
  - ✓ little or no understanding of audience
  - ✓ a weak ability to relate a sequence of events and their significance to the audience
  - ✓ infrequent use of concrete sensory details to describe the sights, sounds, and smells of a scene
  - ✓ little variation in sentence type; use of basic, predictable descriptive language
  - ✓ inconsistent use of English-language conventions. Errors may interfere with the reader's understanding of the narrative.

Biographical or Autobiographical Narrative Holistic Scale (continued)

Score 1

This narrative has a vague introduction and displays no clear purpose. Events are disorganized and their significance is hidden.

- *The writing lacks*
  - ✓ attention to most parts of the writing task
  - ✓ a purpose (or provides only a weak sense of purpose), a focus, and effective organization
  - ✓ an understanding of audience
  - ✓ proficiency in relating a sequence of events to the audience
  - ✓ concrete sensory details to describe the sights, sounds, and smells of a scene
  - ✓ sentence variety and descriptive vocabulary
  - ✓ a basic understanding of English-language conventions. Numerous errors often interfere with the reader's understanding of the narrative.

NAME _____ CLASS _____ DATE _____

STUDENT MODEL

Autobiographical Narrative: Sample A

PROMPT

Think about an incident in your life that had a significant effect on you. Then, write an autobiographical narrative about the incident, relating a sequence of events and their significance. Remember to use concrete sensory details to describe the events.

"You know, owning a truck is a big responsibility," my dad said to me, as he wrote a check and handed it to the man selling us the truck. "I'll pay for the truck, but you'll have to take care of the gas and insurance."

One of the best things about my seventeenth summer was getting that pickup truck. It was old and rusty and needed paint, but it ran well and had a great sound system. I needed a job, though, to keep my truck on the road. When a friend told me he was earning seven dollars an hour by talking on a telephone, I quickly applied for a job at the telemarketing firm where he worked. This was not my dream job, but the salary was right.

Two days later I was interrupting family dinners on behalf of a well-known charitable organization. Along with other telemarketers, I sat in a large, dingy room that smelled of stale coffee and industrial cleaners. Around this room in small, somewhat nicer offices sat the managers. As I made calls, these managers took turns listening in, offering tips such as "Sound friendlier on your opening pitch" or "Pursue the pledge." Day by day I became more confident and successful. My pledges increased steadily. The managers complimented me on my progress. I didn't like the work much, but the lure of that paycheck kept me coming back.

In my third week, I reached an elderly woman who, after patiently listening to my pitch, informed me that her husband had just died and that she had just been involved in a serious auto accident. She apologized for not being able to pledge. I offered her my sympathies and hung up, feeling sorry to have disturbed her. You would have

Autobiographical Narrative: Sample A (continued)

thought I had killed Flipper! A manager appeared at my side, saying that if I didn't pursue the pledge, I would be fired. "You can't afford to be nice in this business," he growled.

I quit on the spot. While I always knew I would go to college, this experience cemented my resolve to prepare for a more meaningful career. I do not want to have to settle for a job just because it pays the bills—a job like that seven-dollar-per-hour telemarketing gig.

At this point, I'm earning minimum wage at a pizza joint. I can't afford to buy as much gas as I could at seven dollars per hour, but now I serve dinner instead of interrupting it.

FOR THE TEACHER

SCORING

Autobiographical Narrative Sample A Evaluation

Holistic Scale

Rating: 4 points

Note: This essay illustrates the type of development appropriate for the prompt, but some teachers may ask their students for longer essays.

Comments: This is a thoughtful autobiographical narrative that shows a thorough understanding of all aspects of the writing task. The reader is drawn into the narrative by interesting dialogue in the introduction. The narrative is well organized and purposeful, with concrete sensory details describing the sequence of events. The significance of the events is clearly communicated in the fifth paragraph. Tone and focus are consistent and appropriate. Sentences are varied and clear in meaning. The narrative shows a solid command of English-language conventions.

Analytical Scale: 7 Writing Traits

Ratings (High score is 5.)
Ideas and Content: 4   **Sentence Fluency: 5**
Organization: 5   **Conventions: 5**
Voice: 5   **Presentation: 4**
Word Choice: 4

Comments:

Ideas and Content: Personal work experience is used to relate an interesting sequence of events that significantly affected the writer's career plans. Vivid details help the reader visualize the events and convey their significance.

Organization: Dialogue helps grab the reader's interest. The sequence of events is presented logically. The narrative has a clever and satisfying conclusion.

Voice: The tone is appropriate for an autobiographical narrative. A personal dimension is revealed throughout the essay, and the point of view is sincere and compelling.

Word Choice: The narrative's language is natural. Vivid sensory details help create distinct images in the reader's mind. Words are specific and appropriate.

Sentence Fluency: Sentences are clear in meaning and are varied in length and structure. Transitions help the reader understand relationships between ideas. Dialogue is used naturally and purposefully.

Conventions: Effective paragraphing enhances the essay's organization, and the writer demonstrates a strong command of English-language conventions.

Presentation: The presentation is simple and clear.

Autobiographical Narrative: Sample B

STUDENT MODEL

> **PROMPT**
>
> Think about an incident in your life that had a significant effect on you. Then, write an autobiographical narrative about the incident, relating a sequence of events and their significance. Remember to use concrete sensory details to describe the events.

As my dad wrote a check for my first truck and handed it to the man selling us the truck, he reminded me of the responsibilities involved. "I'll pay for the truck, but you'll have to take care of the gas and insurance", he said.

One of the best things about my seventeenth summer was getting that pickup truck. I needed a job though to keep my truck on the road. When a friend told me he was earning seven dollars an hour by talking on a telephone, I quickly applied for a job at the telemarketing firm where he worked.

Two days later I was interupting family dinners on behalf of a well known charitable organization. Along with other telemarketers, I sat in a room surrounded by the offices of managers. As I made calls these managers took turns listening in and offering tips. Day by day I became more confident and succesful. My pledges increased steadily. The managers complemented me on my progress. I didn't like the work much, but the lure of that paycheck kept me coming back.

In my third week, I reached an elderly woman who said she couldn't pledge because her husband had just died and she had just been involved in a car accident. I offered her my sympathies and hung up. A manager came and told me that if I didn't pursue the pledge I would be fired.

I quit on the spot. I always knew I would go to college, but this incident had such an effect on me that I became even more serious about preparing for a meaningful career. I do not want to have to settle for a job just because it pays the bills—a job like that seven-dollar-per-hour telemarketing gig.

FOR THE TEACHER

SCORING

Autobiographical Narrative Sample B Evaluation

Holistic Scale

Rating: 3 points

Comments: This autobiographical narrative shows a general understanding of the writing task. The narrative is well organized, and the significance of the events is clearly communicated in the fifth paragraph. Tone and focus are appropriate. Sentences are varied and clear in meaning. The narrative shows a good understanding of English-language conventions.

Analytical Scale: 7 Writing Traits

Ratings (High score is 5.)

Ideas and Content: 3	**Sentence Fluency:** 3
Organization: 4	**Conventions:** 3
Voice: 3	**Presentation:** 4
Word Choice: 3	

Comments:

Ideas and Content: Personal work experience is used to relate a sequence of events that significantly affected the writer's career plans. More details are needed to support the main idea.

Organization: Sentences and paragraphs flow smoothly and logically, presenting the sequence of events in chronological order.

Voice: The tone is appropriate for an autobiographical narrative, though somewhat flat. A personal dimension is revealed, but concrete sensory details are needed to add color and clarify the significance of the events.

Word Choice: The narrative's language is natural. Words are specific and appropriate.

Sentence Fluency: Sentences are clear in meaning and vary in structure, but they lack flair. Transitions help the reader understand relationships between ideas.

Conventions: The narrative shows a good understanding of English-language conventions, but a few minor errors exist in spelling and punctuation.

Presentation: The presentation is simple and clear.

Autobiographical Narrative: Sample C

STUDENT MODEL

> **PROMPT**
>
> Think about an incident in your life that had a significant effect on you. Then, write an autobiographical narrative about the incident, relating a sequence of events and their significance. Remember to use concrete sensory details to describe the events.

For my first truck my dad wrote a check and handed it to the man. He reminded me that I needed to buy gas and stuff for the truck.

I got a pickup truck when I was seventeen. That was one of the best things. I needed to get money for gas though. A friend told me he was getting seven dollars an hour by talking on a telephone and I applied for a job there.

One time I was talking to a elderly woman who said she couldn't pledge. She said it was because her husband had just died and she had just been in a wreck. I felt so bad so I hung up. A manager told me he'd fire me if I didn't try to get that money out of her.

I started work just two days after I made that application. I sat in a room surrounded by the offices of managers. They took turns listening in and offering tips. I got pretty good and so I was getting lots of pledges. The bosses even had told me I was doing real good. I didn't like the work, but I needed money for gas for my truck or else I couldnt drive it.

Now I deliver pizza. It is more fun even though some people are jerks. It don't pay nearly as much money but now I can feel good about my work and I get to drive my truck too.

FOR THE TEACHER

Autobiographical Narrative Sample C Evaluation

SCORING

Holistic Scale

Rating: 2 points

Comments: This autobiographical narrative shows a limited understanding of the writing task. The third paragraph should follow the fourth paragraph for logical progression, and the significance of the events is unclear. The tone is generally consistent and appropriate, but the topic is unfocused and poorly developed. Sentences are clear in meaning but lack variety in length and structure. The narrative shows a general understanding of English-language conventions.

Analytical Scale: 7 Writing Traits

Ratings (High score is 5.)
Ideas and Content: 2   **Sentence Fluency: 2**
Organization: 1   **Conventions: 3**
Voice: 3   **Presentation: 4**
Word Choice: 2

Comments:

Ideas and Content: The introduction is vague, and its relationship to the rest of the narrative is unclear. The significance of the events is not specified. The narrative lacks development.

Organization: Ideas are not presented in chronological order.

Voice: The tone is generally sincere but is very flat and monotonous.

Word Choice: The narrative's language is natural. Words are general and basic rather than specific.

Sentence Fluency: Sentences are generally clear in meaning, but they lack variety in length and structure. Transitions are needed to help the reader understand relationships between ideas.

Conventions: The narrative shows a general understanding of English-language conventions, but errors exist in grammar, spelling, and punctuation.

Presentation: The presentation is simple and clear.

Exposition: Holistic Scale

Score 4

This expository writing presents a clear thesis or controlling impression and supports it with precise, relevant evidence.

- *The writing strongly demonstrates*
  - ✓ a clear understanding of all parts of the writing task
  - ✓ a meaningful thesis or controlling impression, a consistent tone and focus, and a purposeful control of organization
  - ✓ use of specific details and examples to support the main ideas
  - ✓ a variety of sentence types using precise, descriptive language
  - ✓ a clear understanding of audience
  - ✓ inclusion of accurate information from all relevant perspectives
  - ✓ anticipation of and thorough attention to readers' possible misunderstandings, biases, and expectations
  - ✓ a solid command of English-language conventions. Errors, if any, are generally minor and unobstrusive.

Score 3

This expository writing presents a thesis or controlling impression and supports it with evidence.

- *The writing generally demonstrates*
  - ✓ an understanding of all parts of the writing task
  - ✓ a thesis or controlling impression, a consistent tone and focus, and a control of organization
  - ✓ use of details and examples to support the main ideas
  - ✓ a variety of sentence types using some descriptive language
  - ✓ an understanding of audience
  - ✓ inclusion of accurate information from relevant perspectives
  - ✓ anticipation of and attention to readers' possible misunderstandings, biases, and expectations
  - ✓ an understanding of English-language conventions. Some errors exist, but they do not interfere with the reader's understanding.

Score 2

This expository writing presents a thesis or controlling impression, but the thesis is not sufficiently supported.

- *The writing demonstrates*
  - ✓ an understanding of only parts of the writing task
  - ✓ a thesis or controlling impression (though not always); an inconsistent tone and focus; and little, if any, control of organization
  - ✓ use of limited, if any, details and examples to support the main ideas
  - ✓ little variation in sentence types; use of basic, predictable language
  - ✓ little or no understanding of audience
  - ✓ little or no inclusion of information from relevant perspectives
  - ✓ little, if any, anticipation of and attention to readers' possible misunderstandings, biases, and expectations

Scales and Sample Papers

Exposition: Holistic Scale (continued)

	✓ inconsistent use of English-language conventions. Several errors exist and may interfere with the reader's understanding.
Score 1 **This expository writing may present a thesis or controlling impression, but it is not supported.**	▪ *The writing lacks* ✓ an understanding of the writing task, addressing only one part ✓ a thesis or controlling impression (or provides only a weak one), a focus, and control of organization ✓ details and examples to support ideas ✓ sentence variety and adequate vocabulary ✓ an understanding of audience ✓ accurate information from relevant perspectives ✓ anticipation of and attention to readers' possible misunderstandings, biases, and expectations ✓ an understanding of English-language conventions. Serious errors interfere with the reader's understanding.

STUDENT MODEL

Exposition: Sample A

> **PROMPT**
>
> Has a particular landscape had a significant effect on you? What about a person or even an object? Write a descriptive essay about the person, place, or thing of your choice. Remember to include concrete sensory details that develop a controlling impression.

Wolf or dog? That's the first thing that might pop into your head when you see my enormous Alaskan malamute, Drifter. The next thing you might wonder—and quick on the heels of your first thought—is whether this beast is friend or foe. When Drifter meets someone for the first time, and sometimes for the second and third, he strikes a pose that would make White Fang jealous. He bares his long, menacing canines under snarled lips, and, odd as it may sound, he rumbles like a freight train. That's the best way I can describe his low, steady growl. As frightening as Drifter may sound, however, at heart he's a big, playful baby.

Drifter has a coal-black nose with a touch of pink on the tip. Whether he was born with that pink mark as a sign of his true inner tenderness or acquired it some other way, I can't be sure. It was that way when I found him as a puppy, wandering alone in a blizzard several years ago. Drifter immediately became my constant companion and has done his best to earn the reputation of man's best friend. At least, he's my best friend.

The markings around Drifter's mouth seem to form a clownlike smile, especially when he playfully opens his jaws, his large, pink tongue lolling to one side. As with most Alaskan huskies and malamutes, Drifter's masked face lends a dashing air to his appearance. But, as if the goofy "grin" weren't enough, Drifter is betrayed by a cap of furry, blunted ears that look rather too small for his huge head even when they stand erect.

Drifter's thick coat is a luscious gray and white, darkening toward his hindquarters. His hair is so thick that when he sheds in the spring, our back yard begins to resemble

Scales and Sample Papers **83**

Exposition: Sample A *(continued)*

a cotton field, with fuzzy, white "bolls" of hair blowing around like tumbleweeds. Once unfrocked, Drifter is fond of chasing his newly shed winter coat around the yard on especially windy spring days.

    Drifter's muscular chest and front legs give him a triangular shape; he seems to taper from head to tail like a caricature of a Spanish fighting bull. When he's tearing around our fenced back yard, it isn't too much of a stretch to imagine him entering the ring in Pamplona. "Toro! Toro!" I yell as he circles the yard, loose dirt flying from his hind paws. But much to Drifter's chagrin, I'm sure, his bushy, slightly curled, and always wagging tail reveals his true identity—and his true nature.

FOR THE TEACHER

SCORING

Exposition: Sample A Evaluation

Holistic Scale

Rating: 4 points

Note: This essay illustrates the type of development appropriate for the prompt, but some teachers may ask their students for longer essays.

Comments: This expository writing grabs the reader's attention with an interesting opening, presents a clear thesis, and supports the thesis with concrete sensory details and examples. The tone is appropriate, and the paper is logically organized, describing the dog from head to tail. The potential bias against big dogs is sufficiently addressed. Sentences are varied and clear, and the writing shows a strong command of English-language conventions.

Analytical Scale: 7 Writing Traits

Ratings (High score is 5.)
Ideas and Content: 4   **Sentence Fluency:** 5
Organization: 5   **Conventions:** 5
Voice: 4   **Presentation:** 4
Word Choice: 5

Comments:

Ideas and Content: The paper is clearly focused, and the writer is obviously writing from personal experience. The topic is purposeful, and the possible bias against big dogs is addressed.

Organization: The paper has an attention-grabbing opening and a clear thesis. Organization is clear and logical.

Voice: The tone is appropriate, and the writing reveals a personal dimension without becoming too informal.

Word Choice: The writing shows careful attention to word choice. The language is natural, while revealing a varied vocabulary.

Sentence Fluency: A variety of sentence types are used. Sentence construction makes the writing easy to read.

Conventions: The writer demonstrates a strong command of English-language conventions.

Presentation: The presentation is simple and clear.

Scales and Sample Papers **85**

STUDENT MODEL

Exposition: Sample B

> **PROMPT**
>
> Has a particular landscape had a significant effect on you? What about a person or even an object? Write a descriptive essay about the person, place, or thing of your choice. Remember to include concrete sensory details that develop a controlling impression.

The first thing you might wonder when you see my enormous Alaskan malamute, Drifter, is weather he is a dog or a wolf. The next thing you might wonder is weather he is mean or friendly. When Drifter meets someone for the first time, and sometimes for the second and third, he acts pretty mean. He snarls his lips, shows his big teeth and odd as it may sound, rumbles like a freight train. That's the best way I can describe his growl. As mean as Drifter may sound, at heart he's a big, playful baby.

Drifter has a black nose with a little mark on the tip. Drifter immediately became my constant companion and has done his best to earn the reputation of man's best friend.

Drifter's mouth looks like it is smiling especially when he open his jaws and hangs his tongue off to the side. Like most malamutes, Drifter looks like he's wearing a mask. He has furry ears that look too small for his head.

Drifters hair is grey and white. It is so thick that when he sheds in the spring, our back-yard has hair all over it. He likes to chase his hair around the yard on windy days.

Drifter has a very strong-looking chest. When he's running around the yard, he looks like a bull in a ring. Dirt even flies from his hind paws. But as mean as Drifter may look at first, his constantly wagging tail gives away his friendly nature.

FOR THE TEACHER

SCORING

Exposition: Sample B Evaluation

Holistic Scale

Rating: 3 points
Comments: This expository writing presents a clear thesis and supports the thesis with details and examples. The tone is appropriate, and the paper is logically organized, describing the dog from head to tail. The potential bias against big dogs is addressed. Sentences are varied and clear, and the writing shows a good command of English-language conventions.

Analytical Scale: 7 Writing Traits

Ratings (High score is 5.)

Ideas and Content: 3	Sentence Fluency: 3
Organization: 4	Conventions: 3
Voice: 3	Presentation: 4
Word Choice: 3	

Comments:

Ideas and Content: The paper is focused, and the writer seems to be writing from personal experience. However, main ideas are not as well developed as they should be.

Organization: The thesis is clear, and ideas are logically organized.

Voice: The tone is appropriate, but the writing is somewhat flat and does not reveal a strong personal dimension.

Word Choice: Word choice is generally adequate but fails to reach beyond the mundane.

Sentence Fluency: A variety of sentence types are used. Better transitions are needed to help clarify relationships between ideas.

Conventions: The writer demonstrates a good command of English-language conventions, but the paper contains errors in spelling and punctuation.

Presentation: The presentation is simple and clear.

Scales and Sample Papers 87

Exposition: Sample C

STUDENT MODEL

> **PROMPT**
>
> Has a particular landscape had a significant effect on you? What about a person or even an object? Write a descriptive essay about the person, place, or thing of your choice. Remember to include concrete sensory details that develop a controlling impression.

When you see my big dog you mite think he's a woolf. You'll get scared cause he acts mean. He grouls and sticks his teeth out at people, then he growls really loudly. But he might sound mean, although he's really not he's really nice.

My dog's name is drifter. He has a black nose with a mark on it. I don't know why its their though. It always was. When I got him it was their!

My dog has a big chest. His legs are really strong too. He can almost knock me down sometime. He runs around the yard and dirt comes up in the air like he was a horse running around the yard. However although he looks mean and could probably hurt you he don't because hes really a nice dog.

His mouth looks funny. He has circles around his eyes too; just like racoons.

His hair is grey and white. Its really thick because it falls out sometimes and its all over the place and I have to pick it up or I get in trouble because Im the one who wanted to keep him. He chased it once. That was funny too.

FOR THE TEACHER

SCORING

Exposition: Sample C Evaluation

Holistic Scale

Rating: 2 points
Comments: This expository writing is vague and poorly developed. Organization is illogical. Sentences are not varied in structure, and the writing shows a poor understanding of English-language conventions.

Analytical Scale: 7 Writing Traits

Ratings (High score is 5.)
Ideas and Content: 1   **Sentence Fluency: 1**
Organization: 2   **Conventions: 2**
Voice: 2   **Presentation: 4**
Word Choice: 2

Comments:
Ideas and Content: The thesis is vague and unsupported. The writing is too brief to adequately develop the topic.
Organization: Ideas do not follow one another logically. All ideas seem to carry equal weight.
Voice: The writer seems to speak in a monotone.
Word Choice: Word choice is basic. The word *really* is used too much.
Sentence Fluency: Sentences vary little in structure. Transitions are needed. The last paragraph contains a run-on sentence.
Conventions: The writer demonstrates a poor understanding of English-language conventions. The paper contains serious errors in spelling, grammar, and punctuation.
Presentation: The presentation is simple and clear.

Response to Literature: Holistic Scale

Score 4 This insightful response to literature presents a thoroughly supported thesis and illustrates a comprehensive grasp of the text and the author's use of literary devices.	■ *The writing strongly demonstrates* ✓ a thoughtful, comprehensive understanding of the text ✓ support of the thesis and main ideas with specific textual details and examples that are accurate and coherent ✓ a thorough understanding of the text's ambiguities, nuances, and complexities ✓ a variety of sentence types using precise, descriptive language ✓ a clear understanding of the author's use of literary and stylistic devices ✓ a solid command of English-language conventions. Errors, if any, are generally minor and unobtrusive.
Score 3 This response to literature presents a clear thesis that is supported by details and examples.	■ *The writing generally demonstrates* ✓ a comprehensive understanding of the text ✓ support of the thesis and main ideas with general textual details and examples that are accurate and coherent ✓ an understanding of the text's ambiguities, nuances, and complexities ✓ a variety of sentence types using some descriptive language ✓ an understanding of the author's use of literary and stylistic devices ✓ an understanding of English-language conventions. Some errors exist, but they do not interfere with the reader's understanding of the essay.
Score 2 This literary response presents a thesis, but it is not sufficiently supported. The writing shows little understanding of the text.	■ *The writing demonstrates* ✓ a limited understanding of the text ✓ little, if any, support of the thesis and main ideas with textual details and examples ✓ limited, or no, understanding of the text's ambiguities, nuances, and complexities ✓ little variety in sentence types; use of basic, predictable language ✓ a limited understanding of the author's use of literary and stylistic devices ✓ inconsistent use of English-language conventions. Several errors exist and may interfere with the reader's understanding of the essay.

SCALES AND SAMPLE PAPERS

Holt Assessment: Writing, Listening, and Speaking

Response to Literature: Holistic Scale *(continued)*

Score 1

This literary response contains serious analytical and English-language errors. It shows no understanding of the text or of the author's use of literary devices.

- *The writing lacks*
  - ✓ a comprehensive understanding of the text
  - ✓ textual details and examples to support the thesis and main ideas
  - ✓ an understanding of the text's ambiguities, nuances, and complexities
  - ✓ sentence variety and adequate vocabulary
  - ✓ an understanding of the author's use of literary and stylistic devices
  - ✓ an understanding of English-language conventions. Serious errors interfere with the reader's understanding of the essay.

STUDENT MODEL

Response to Literature: Sample A

> **PROMPT**
>
> Your class has studied great nineteenth-century American novelists, such as Herman Melville, Henry James, and Mark Twain. Think of a novel you have read, and write a literary analysis of the novel to share with your class. Remember to focus on the literary and stylistic devices the author uses throughout the novel.

Mark Twain's _Adventures of Huckleberry Finn_ chronicles the Mississippi River journey of two runaways—Huck, who is running from his abusive father, and Jim, a man who is escaping slavery. The novel examines the theme of nature versus civilization. Huck Finn is a natural, down-to-earth character who feels separated from society. Widow Douglas is trying to civilize Huck, and he blames himself for being ignorant and ornery. However, Twain shows that Huck's naturalness is redeeming and that his harsh criticism of himself is really a criticism of society.

Early in the novel, the mighty Mississippi River is established as a major symbol of the natural world and what it provides. The river offers Huck a means of escape from his father. Huck walks along the bank keeping an eye out for his father and for anything that might be of use, and he finds a canoe. Later, the river provides a raft and supplies for Huck and Jim to begin their journey.

Twain illustrates the superiority of nature over civilization through Huck and Jim's life together on the raft. Huck has been raised to consider Jim inferior to himself. His social conscience, which symbolizes civilization, tells him that people would call him an abolitionist for not turning Jim in to the authorities. Huck overcomes his acquired prejudice, however; his decision to help Jim shows his natural concern for another human being and his innate respect for human dignity. Huck and Jim live peacefully and cooperatively on the raft, floating down the river.

Response to Literature: Sample A (continued)

When the action of the novel takes place on land (a symbol of civilization), events are more sinister. On land, Huck and Jim encounter con men, thieves, and many other unpleasant characters. While Huck is staying with the Grangerford family, for example, the family's long-standing feud with the Shepherdsons escalates and ends in slaughter. Unlike the negative aspects of civilization on land, life on the river is helpful and compassionate.

The novel's conclusion shows that the river journey with Jim has allowed Huck's natural self to, in part, defeat civilization's negative pull on him. He can no longer accept the conflicts and contradictions of civilized society. The novel ends with Huck planning to head for the Western Territory because another woman has plans to adopt and civilize him.

Twain uses the river journey to show the struggle between the demands of civilized society and the instinctive goodness of the natural world. Huck wrestles to the end with the war between his conscience and society's requirements. Finally we see, along with Huck, that he is most comfortable when he is on the real and the metaphorical river, following his naturally open and honest heart.

FOR THE TEACHER

Response to Literature: Sample A Evaluation

SCORING

Holistic Scale

Rating: 4 points

Note: This essay illustrates the type of development appropriate for the prompt, but some teachers may ask their students for longer essays.

Comments: This response to literature is thorough and thoughtful, showing a comprehensive understanding of the novel. The thesis is clearly stated and is well supported by the main ideas. Relevant and accurate textual details and examples are used throughout the analysis as supporting evidence for the thesis and main points. The writer perceptively cites the novelist's use of symbolism, such as the river. Sentences are well written and varied in structure, and English-language conventions are strictly observed.

Analytical Scale: 7 Writing Traits

Ratings (High score is 5.)

Ideas and Content: 5
Organization: 5
Voice: 5
Word Choice: 5
Sentence Fluency: 5
Conventions: 5
Presentation: 4

Comments:

Ideas and Content: The topic is purposeful and thoroughly developed. Details are insightful and well considered.

Organization: Ideas are presented logically and effectively. The analysis has a clear introduction and thoughtful conclusion.

Voice: The tone is somewhat formal and academic, though appropriate for a serious discussion of a novel.

Word Choice: The writer has chosen words carefully, striving for precision rather than generalities.

Sentence Fluency: Sentences are varied and well constructed. The analysis is easy to read, with sentences that flow smoothly and contain thoughtful transitions.

Conventions: The writing shows an excellent command of grammar, usage, and mechanics.

Presentation: The presentation is simple and clear.

NAME _____ CLASS _____ DATE _____

STUDENT MODEL

Response to Literature: Sample B

> **PROMPT**
>
> Your class has studied great nineteenth-century American novelists, such as Herman Melville, Henry James, and Mark Twain. Think of a novel you have read, and write a literary analysis of the novel to share with your class. Remember to focus on the literary and stylistic devices the author uses throughout the novel.

Mark Twain's famous novel, <u>The Adventures of Huckleberry Finn</u>, relates a tale about a trip down the Mississippi River by two runaways—Huck who is running from his abusive father, and Jim, a runaway slave. The novel's theme puts nature against so-called civilization.

Early in the novel the mighty Mississippi is established as a major symbol of the natural world. The River provides good things for Huck and Jim. Later the River provides a raft and supplies for Huck and Jim to begin their journey.

Twain seems to think nature is better than civilization and he shows that through Huck and Jim's life together on the raft. Huck has been raised to consider slaves as being inferior. His civilized social conscience tells him that people would call him an abolitionist for not turning Jim in to the authorities. Huck and Jim live peacefully and cooperatively on the raft, floating down the River. Huck tells Jim that he wouldn't want to be anywhere else.

When the action of the novel takes place on land, which symbolizes civilization, the events are unhappy. On land Huck and Jim meet con men, thieves, and many other unpleasant people. On the River life is helpful and compassionate because there was friendliness on the raft.

Twain uses the River journey to show the struggle between the demands of civilized society and the natural world. In the end we see that Huck is most comfortable when he is on the River, both real and metaphorical.

FOR THE TEACHER

SCORING

Response to Literature: Sample B Evaluation

Holistic Scale

Rating: 3 points

Comments: This response to literature shows a general understanding of the novel. The thesis is clear and is supported by the main ideas. Limited textual details and examples support the thesis and main points. The writer cites the river as a use of symbolism. Sentences are varied in structure, and, with the exception of a few punctuation and capitalization errors, English-language conventions are observed.

Analytical Scale: 7 Writing Traits

Ratings (High score is 5.)

Ideas and Content: 3 **Sentence Fluency:** 3
Organization: 4 **Conventions:** 3
Voice: 4 **Presentation:** 4
Word Choice: 3

Comments:

Ideas and Content: The thesis is well focused, but limited textual details and examples support the thesis and main ideas.

Organization: Organization is clear, logical, and effective. The introduction clearly states the thesis, main ideas are presented logically, and the conclusion restates the thesis and provides a thoughtful closing statement.

Voice: The tone is appropriate, but the writer offers generalities rather than personal insights. There is little attempt to build credibility with the reader.

Word Choice: Words are generally used correctly, but commonplace words are used more often than precise, vivid descriptions.

Sentence Fluency: Sentences are varied in length and grammatically correct, but they are routine rather than artful.

Conventions: The analysis contains some errors in punctuation and capitalization, but sentences are grammatical.

Presentation: The presentation is clear.

STUDENT MODEL

Response to Literature: Sample C

> **PROMPT**
>
> Your class has studied great nineteenth-century American novelists, such as Herman Melville, Henry James, and Mark Twain. Think of a novel you have read, and write a literary analysis of the novel to share with your class. Remember to focus on the literary and stylistic devices the author uses throughout the novel.

This book is about how being on a river in a raft with a good friend is a whole lot better than being around people who are mean. Mark Twain, a.k.a. Sam Clements— wrote a famous novel, called The Adventures of Huckleberry Finn. It tells about a trip down the Mississippi by a boy and a run-away slave.

The river gives good things for Huck and Jim. They later on get a raft and stuff for there journey write out of the water

He seems to think nature is better than the modern word and he shows that by all the fun they have on the boat. Huck has always thought slaves were worse than him so he says people would call him an abolitionist for not turning Jim into the cops. But Huck likes Jim. Once, he said it was nice to be with him. At the end Huck was planning to go to the Western Territory

When theyre on land, where people are civilized, bad things are always happning. They run into con men robbers, and many other bad people. On the River life is great.

I like the way they talk just like normal people and he didn't try to make them sound like they wouldn't have. That it the real sign of a great writer.

Scales and Sample Papers **97**

FOR THE TEACHER

SCORING

Response to Literature: Sample C Evaluation

Holistic Scale

Rating: 2 points
Comments: This analysis shows a lack of understanding of both the writing task and the novel. The introduction presents a vague and poorly considered thesis. Little support is provided for the thesis and main ideas. The writer clearly does not understand the author's use of literary and stylistic devices.

Analytical Scale: 7 Writing Traits

Ratings (High score is 5.)
Ideas and Content: 2   **Sentence Fluency: 2**
Organization: 2   **Conventions: 2**
Voice: 3   **Presentation: 3**
Word Choice: 3

Comments:
Ideas and Content: The analysis shows superficial understanding of the novel. The thesis is inappropriate and incorrect. Little detail exists to support the thesis and main ideas.
Organization: The analysis has an introduction, but it is unsupported. Ideas do not flow logically. There is no conclusion.
Voice: The tone is generally appropriate, though sometimes rather informal.
Word Choice: The language is simple and generally clear.
Sentence Fluency: There is little variety in sentence structure, and missing transitions impair readability and comprehension. Several pronouns have unclear antecedents.
Conventions: The analysis contains serious errors in punctuation, spelling, and capitalization.
Presentation: The presentation is clear.

SCALES AND SAMPLE PAPERS

98   Holt Assessment: Writing, Listening, and Speaking

Persuasion: Holistic Scale

Score 4

This persuasive writing presents a clear position and supports the position with precise, relevant evidence. The reader's concerns, biases, and expectations are addressed convincingly.

- **The writing strongly demonstrates**
  - ✓ a clear understanding of all parts of the writing task
  - ✓ a meaningful thesis, a consistent tone and focus, and a purposeful control of organization
  - ✓ use of specific details and examples to support the thesis and main ideas
  - ✓ a variety of sentence types using precise, descriptive language
  - ✓ a clear understanding of audience
  - ✓ use of precise, relevant evidence to defend a position with authority, convincingly addressing the reader's concerns, biases, and expectations
  - ✓ a solid command of English-language conventions. Errors, if any, are generally minor and unobtrusive.

Score 3

This persuasive writing presents a position and supports it with evidence. The reader's concerns are addressed.

- **The writing generally demonstrates**
  - ✓ an understanding of all parts of the writing task
  - ✓ a thesis, a consistent tone and focus, and a control of organization
  - ✓ use of details and examples to support the thesis and main ideas
  - ✓ a variety of sentence types using some descriptive language
  - ✓ an understanding of audience
  - ✓ use of relevant evidence to defend a position, addressing the reader's concerns, biases, and expectations
  - ✓ an understanding of English-language conventions. Some errors exist, but they do not interfere with the reader's understanding of the essay.

Score 2

This persuasive writing presents a position, but the position is not sufficiently supported.

- **The writing demonstrates**
  - ✓ an understanding of only parts of the writing task
  - ✓ a thesis (though not always); an inconsistent tone and focus; and little, if any, control of organization
  - ✓ use of limited, if any, details and examples to support the thesis and main ideas
  - ✓ little variety in sentence types; use of basic, predictable language
  - ✓ little or no understanding of audience
  - ✓ use of little, if any, evidence to defend a position. The reader's concerns, biases, and expectations are not effectively addressed.
  - ✓ inconsistent use of English-language conventions. Several errors exist and may interfere with the reader's understanding of the essay.

Persuasion: Holistic Scale *(continued)*

Score 1

This persuasive writing may present a position, but it is not supported.

- *The writing lacks*
  - ✓ an understanding of the writing task, addressing only one part
  - ✓ a thesis (or provides only a weak thesis), a focus, and control of organization
  - ✓ details and examples to support ideas
  - ✓ sentence variety and uses limited vocabulary
  - ✓ an understanding of audience
  - ✓ evidence to defend a position and fails to address the reader's concerns, biases, and expectations
  - ✓ an understanding of English-language conventions. Serious errors interfere with the reader's understanding of the essay.

Persuasion: Sample A

STUDENT MODEL

PROMPT

Have you ever tried to persuade a friend or family member to see things your way? Think of an issue you feel strongly about, and write a persuasive essay for your school newspaper using relevant evidence to defend your position. Be sure to address possible reader biases in your essay.

After basketball practice, I often head straight for the vending machines in the locker room to buy my favorite soft drink. It's no accident that all the soft drinks dispensed by this machine are produced by the same company and that the company's logo is emblazoned on the machines, on the new electronic scoreboard, and inside the school lobby. A contract between the school and a soft drink company has made this possible. Some people oppose the renewal of this contract because it allows such advertising to be placed in the school. However, I feel that the contract has provided the school with some badly needed revenue.

Let's face it: with its peeling paint and cramped quarters, Harrisonville High needs the money that the contract generates. Although expenses and enrollment have soared, the state has failed to fund schools adequately in recent years. In contrast, the last contract between Harrisonville and the soft drink company provided money, equipment, and materials. Because of this contract, I have conducted sophisticated experiments in my physics class and dribbled my basketball across a new gym floor.

What did the soft drink company receive in return for its money? The contract gave it exclusive rights to sell its products at school and at school functions as well as the right to use its logo in the school. In other words, the company gained a captive audience for its ads and an opportunity to establish name recognition for its products.

Some people feel that this form of marketing in schools may influence students' purchasing patterns. I don't agree that the company's ads will unduly influence students to buy the products of the company. Students are constantly bombarded

Persuasion: Sample A *(continued)*

by advertisements everywhere they go. They see labels on clothing and shoes, watch commercials on television, and view ads on the Internet. Ads are so prevalent outside the school that the ones inside the school are barely noticeable.

  A new contract with the soft drink company will provide even more benefits to the school. It can help the school achieve its goal of providing students a top-notch education, which in turn will benefit the community as a whole. Encourage your friends to contact members of the school board in support of this important source of revenue for the school.

FOR THE TEACHER

SCORING

Persuasion: Sample A Evaluation

Holistic Scale

Rating: 4 points

Note: This sample illustrates the type of development appropriate for the prompt, but some teachers may ask their students for longer essays.

Comments: This is a well-written, thoroughly developed persuasive essay. The introduction presents the issue in a way that is interesting and easy to understand. The thesis is clear and is supported by relevant main points. Specific details and examples provide strong support for the thesis and main ideas. The possible reader bias against advertising in schools is addressed. The essay's tone is consistent and appropriate for an audience of high school peers. The writing shows a strong command of English-language conventions.

Analytical Scale: 7 Writing Traits

Ratings (High score is 5.)
Ideas and Content: 5 **Sentence Fluency: 4**
Organization: 5 **Conventions: 5**
Voice: 4 **Presentation: 4**
Word Choice: 4

Comments:
Ideas and Content: The topic is clearly focused, and the writer seems to be writing from personal experience. Development of the topic is thorough and purposeful. The writer anticipates and addresses possible biases.

Organization: The sequence of ideas is logical. The essay contains an inviting introduction and a clear conclusion that includes a specific call to action. Transitions are used effectively to connect ideas.

Voice: The tone is consistent and appropriate for the audience. The writing reveals a personal dimension and explains why the reader should care about the issue.

Word Choice: Word choice is specific and effective.

Sentence Fluency: Sentences are clear and well constructed, varying in length and structure.

Conventions: The writing shows an excellent command of English-language conventions.

Presentation: The presentation is simple and clear.

Scales and Sample Papers **103**

Persuasion: Sample B

STUDENT MODEL

PROMPT

Have you ever tried to persuade a friend or family member to see things your way? Think of an issue you feel strongly about, and write a persuasive essay for your school newspaper using relevant evidence to defend your position. Be sure to address possible reader biases in your essay.

After basketball practice I usually run to the locker room and grab a soft drink with the guys. But wait, all the soft drinks are made by the same company! Now that I think of it, that same company's logo is plastered on the machines, on the new electronic scoreboard, and inside the school lobby. Well, that's no mere coincidence. A contract between the school and the soft drink company has made this possible. Some people say we shouldn't renew the contract because it allows advertising in the school. However, the contract has provided the school with some badly needed revenue.

Let's face it, with its peeling paint and cramped quarters, Harrisonville High needs the money big time. Although expenses and enrollment have soared, the state has let us down by not adequately funding schools. In contrast, the last contract between Harrisonville and the soft drink company provided money, equipment, and materials.

What did the soft drink company receive in return for its money? The contract gave it rights to sell its products at school and at school functions as well as the right to use its logo in the school. Some people feel that this form of marketing in schools may influence students' purchasing patterns. I don't agree that the company's ads will unduly influence students to buy the products of the company.

A new contract with the soft drink company will help the school achieve its goal of providing students a top-notch education.

FOR THE TEACHER

Persuasion: Sample B Evaluation

SCORING

Holistic Scale

Rating: 3 points

Comments: This persuasive essay has a clear thesis that is supported by main points. The possible reader bias against advertising in the school is mentioned but not adequately addressed. The essay's tone is generally appropriate for an audience of high school peers, but it is somewhat inconsistent; the essay begins with an informal tone and becomes more formal toward the end. The writing shows a strong command of English-language conventions.

Analytical Scale: 7 Writing Traits

Ratings (High score is 5.)

Ideas and Content: 3   Sentence Fluency: 4
Organization: 3   Conventions: 5
Voice: 3   Presentation: 4
Word Choice: 3

Comments:

Ideas and Content: The thesis is clear but lacks thorough development and support. Details and examples do not sufficiently explain reasons or evidence, and the possible reader bias is not adequately addressed.

Organization: The essay has a clear introduction, main points, and conclusion. The sequence of ideas is logical. However, the conclusion lacks a call to action.

Voice: The tone is appropriate but inconsistent. The first two paragraphs are quite informal, using phrases such as "grab a soft drink with the guys" and "needs the money big time." The remainder of the essay is more formal.

Word Choice: Words are correct and accurate.

Sentence Fluency: Sentences are varied in length and structure. Transitions are used effectively, and sentences are clear and grammatical.

Conventions: The essay shows a strong command of English-language conventions.

Presentation: The presentation is clear.

STUDENT MODEL

Persuasion: Sample C

> **PROMPT**
>
> Have you ever tried to persuade a friend or family member to see things your way? Think of an issue you feel strongly about, and write a persuasive essay for your school newspaper using relevant evidence to defend your position. Be sure to address possible reader biases in your essay.

After practising hoops I always stroll to the locker room and grab myself a cool drink. I slam it down and then sometimes I grab me another one. Our school have a contract with the company thats making the soda, so we got there cool logo all over the place not just on the machine. We even got it on the new scoreboard they give us. That's why we got that new scoreboard and the fixed-up floor. Coach says hes going to get us some more money from shoe companys and we can have there logo even on our jerzy.

It's a good thing for all these companys giving us money cause the state don't give us no money for stuff like new scoreboards and floors and jerzys.

If you can believe it, some people is complaining cause they think well only buy the stuff that's on them advertizemints in school. I don't no wheir they could start thinking like that because we get to see ads all over the place on TV and sport magazines and even on computers.

The more contracts we can get with these companys the better cause we can keep getting new sports stuff that's really what this school need is to get some school spirit coach is always saying. Then the best players can make the dream come true and go onto play pro hoops and then the school will really have something to chear about. Maybe I'll give the school some money when Im a superstar, but I ain't coming back here you better believe.

FOR THE TEACHER

SCORING

Persuasion: Sample C Evaluation

Holistic Scale

Rating: 2 points
Comments: The writer does not understand the writing task. The thesis of this persuasive essay is vague and is not contained in the introduction. Little supporting evidence is provided for the thesis. The writer mentions a bias against advertising in school but seems to misunderstand the issue. The writing shows a very poor understanding of English-language conventions.

Analytical Scale: 7 Writing Traits

Ratings (High score is 5.)
Ideas and Content: 2   **Sentence Fluency:** 2
Organization: 2   **Conventions:** 2
Voice: 2   **Presentation:** 4
Word Choice: 2

Comments:
Ideas and Content: The thesis is vague and unsupported. The text is both rambling and undeveloped. A possible reader bias is given superficial attention, and there is little subordination of ideas.

Organization: The introduction is confusing, leaving the thesis uncertain. Little evidence exists to support the thesis. The conclusion contains no call to action. Ideas do not progress logically through the essay.

Voice: The tone is too informal, and the writer seems to speak in a monotone. No concern for audience is apparent.

Word Choice: The language is basic and vague.

Sentence Fluency: Sentences are varied in length and structure, and meaning is generally clear. However, the essay contains some run-on sentences.

Conventions: The essay contains serious errors in grammar, spelling, and punctuation.

Presentation: The presentation is clear.

Business Letter: Holistic Scale

Score 4

This business letter provides clear, purposeful information. Conventional business-letter style contributes to readability and overall effect. The tone is consistent and appropriate for the intended audience.

- *The writing strongly demonstrates*
  - ✓ a clear understanding of all parts of the writing task
  - ✓ a meaningful message, a consistent tone and focus, and a purposeful control of organization
  - ✓ use of specific details and examples to support the main purpose
  - ✓ a variety of sentence types using precise, descriptive language
  - ✓ a clear understanding of audience
  - ✓ a thorough understanding of conventional business-letter style, with formats, fonts, and spacing that aid readability and have a positive overall effect
  - ✓ a solid command of English-language conventions. Errors, if any, are minor and unobtrusive.

Score 3

This business letter provides clear information. Conventional business-letter style generally contributes to readability. The tone is appropriate for the intended audience.

- *The writing generally demonstrates*
  - ✓ an understanding of all parts of the writing task
  - ✓ a clear message, a consistent tone and focus, and a control of organization
  - ✓ use of details and examples to support the purpose
  - ✓ a variety of sentence types using some descriptive language
  - ✓ an understanding of audience
  - ✓ an understanding of conventional business-letter style, with formats, fonts, and spacing that aid readability and have a positive overall effect
  - ✓ an understanding of English-language conventions. Some errors exist, but they do not interfere with the reader's understanding of the essay.

Score 2

This business letter provides somewhat vague information and strays from its focus. Conventional business-letter style is not used consistently, leaving a negative overall impression.

- *The writing demonstrates*
  - ✓ an understanding of only parts of the writing task
  - ✓ a weak message; an inconsistent tone and focus; and little, if any, control of organization
  - ✓ use of limited, if any, details and examples to support the purpose
  - ✓ little variety in sentence types and use of basic, predictable language
  - ✓ little or no understanding of audience
  - ✓ little understanding of conventional business-letter style. Formats, fonts, and spacing sometimes impede readability.
  - ✓ inconsistent use of English-language conventions. Several errors exist and may interfere with the reader's understanding of the essay.

Business Letter: Holistic Scale *(continued)*

Score 1

This business letter shows no understanding of business-letter purpose or style. The tone is inappropriate for the audience. Incorrect style and serious grammatical errors greatly impede readability and have an overall negative effect.

- *The writing lacks*
  - ✓ an understanding of the writing task, addressing only one part
  - ✓ a clear message, a focus, and control of organization
  - ✓ details and examples to support ideas
  - ✓ sentence variety and uses limited vocabulary
  - ✓ an understanding of audience
  - ✓ an understanding of conventional business-letter style. Formats, fonts, and spacing impede readability and have a negative overall effect.
  - ✓ an understanding of English-language conventions. Serious errors interfere with the reader's understanding of the essay.

Business Letter: Sample A

STUDENT MODEL

> **PROMPT**
>
> You have probably already had to write a business letter of some form, whether for a college application or a summer job. Using a realistic situation, write a job-application letter using conventional business-letter format.

Jonathan Giacomo
721 Hillside Dr.
Emporia, KS 66801
May 3, 2003

Mr. James Smith, Director
Wattathrill Theme Park
321 Whoopee Ave.
Floor 7
Wichita, KS 67220

Dear Mr. Smith:

I am writing in response to the *Kansas City Star* classified advertisement announcing your openings for summer entertainers at Wattathrill Theme Park. As an accomplished street juggler and mime, I am sure I would be an asset to your summer entertainment, and I would very much appreciate the opportunity to audition for you in person.

I have been juggling since I was in elementary school. I currently perform at children's birthday parties, church festivals, and school fairs. I also have performed in the Kansas City Christmas Parade for the past three years. I juggle rubber balls,

Business Letter: Sample A *(continued)*

bowling pins, and—when my parents are not looking—dishes. My act, "Jugglin' Johnny G," usually includes musical accompaniment in the form of a portable CD player. I like to intersperse some mime work with my juggling routine for variety. I am sure that you are trying to fill positions as quickly as possible, so I am enclosing a video showing a sample of my routines. I would welcome the opportunity to come to Wichita for an audition. My grandmother lives in Wichita, so summer housing would not be a problem.

Thank you very much for your consideration and for taking the time to view my video. I am very excited about the prospect of brightening the faces of children at Wattathrill Theme Park this summer, and I look forward to hearing from you soon.

Sincerely,

Jonathan Giacomo

FOR THE TEACHER

Business Letter: Sample A Evaluation

SCORING

Holistic Scale

Rating: 4 points

Comments: This is a well-written business letter that shows a comprehensive understanding of all parts of business-letter writing. The writer presents a clear purpose and supports it with specific details and examples. The tone is consistent and courteous, though not overly formal; the humorous mention of juggling dishes is appropriate in context. Conventional block-style letter format is used correctly and consistently. Sentences are varied in structure, and the writing shows a strong command of English-language conventions.

Analytical Scale: 7 Writing Traits

Ratings (High score is 5.)
Ideas and Content: 5   **Sentence Fluency:** 4
Organization: 5   **Conventions:** 5
Voice: 4   **Presentation:** 4
Word Choice: 4

Comments:

Ideas and Content: The letter is clearly focused, and the writer is obviously writing from personal experience and knowledge. Development is thorough and purposeful, anticipating and answering readers' questions.

Organization: The letter correctly and consistently uses block-style format. Ideas flow logically.

Voice: While not overly formal, the tone is consistently courteous and is appropriate for the purpose and audience. The writer takes a risk in revealing a humorous personal dimension (juggling dishes while his parents aren't looking).

Word Choice: Words are specific and appropriate. The language is natural.

Sentence Fluency: Sentences are clear in meaning and varied in structure.

Conventions: The letter shows a strong command of English-language conventions.

Presentation: The presentation is simple and clear.

NAME _____ CLASS _____ DATE _____

STUDENT MODEL

Business Letter: Sample B

PROMPT

You have probably already had to write a business letter of some form, whether for a college application or a summer job. Using a realistic situation, write a job-application letter using conventional business-letter format.

Jonathan Giacomo
721 Hillside Dr.
Emporia, KS 66801

Wattathrill Theme Park
321 Whoopee Ave.
Floor 7
Wichita, KS 67220

Dear Wattathrill:

    I am writing in response to the Kansas City Star classified advertisement announcing your openings for summer entertainers at Wattathrill Theme Park. As one of the best street jugglers and mimes in Kansas, I am sure you will want me to help you out with your summer entertainment. Please let me know when I can come audition for you.

    I have been juggling since I was in elementary school. I currently perform at children's birthday parties, church festivals, and school fairs. I also have performed in the Kansas City Christmas Parade for the past three years. I juggle rubber balls, bowling pins, and—when my parents are not looking—dishes. My act, "Jugglin' Johnny G," usually is performed with some tunes from my portable CD player (trust me, it'll shake the ground). I like to intersperse some mime work with my juggling routine for variety; it also gives my arms a rest. My drama coach says I

Scales and Sample Papers 113

Business Letter: Sample B (continued)

am the best mime he has ever seen. I am sure that you are trying to fill positions as quickly as possible, so I am enclosing a video showing a sample of my routines. I would love to cruise over to Wichita in my red coupe for an audition. My grandmother lives in Wichita, so finding a place to stay is a non-issue.

Thank you very much for considering me for this job. Enjoy the video (it's gratis). I'll talk to you soon.

Sincerely,

Jonathan Giacomo

FOR THE TEACHER

SCORING

Business Letter: Sample B Evaluation

Holistic Scale

Rating: 3 points

Comments: This business letter shows a general understanding of all parts of business-letter writing. The writer presents a clear purpose and supports it with specific details and examples. However, the tone is presumptuous and too informal. Conventional block-style letter format is used correctly with the exception of indented paragraphs. Sentences are varied in structure, and the writing shows a strong command of English-language conventions.

Analytical Scale: 7 Writing Traits

Ratings (High score is 5.)

Ideas and Content: 3	**Sentence Fluency:** 3
Organization: 3	**Conventions:** 4
Voice: 2	**Presentation:** 4
Word Choice: 3	

Comments:

Ideas and Content: The letter is generally well focused, though some information, such as "cruise over to Wichita in my red coupe," is inappropriate and superfluous.

Organization: Addressing the company name in the salutation is inappropriate. With the exception of indented paragraphs, block-style format is used consistently.

Voice: The tone is inappropriate for the purpose (requesting an audition) and the audience (a hiring manager). Phrases such as "I am sure you will want me to help you out" and "My drama coach . . ." are presumptuous.

Word Choice: Words are correct and generally adequate. However, use of slang, such as "cruise over" and "it's gratis," is clearly inappropriate for the purpose and audience.

Sentence Fluency: Sentences are clear in meaning and varied in structure.

Conventions: The letter shows a strong command of English-language conventions.

Presentation: The presentation is simple and clear.

Business Letter: Sample C

STUDENT MODEL

> **PROMPT**
> You have probably already had to write a business letter of some form, whether for a college application or a summer job. Using a realistic situation, write a business letter using conventional business-letter format.

Jonathan Giacomo
721 Hillside Dr
Emporia, Kansas 66801

Wattathrill Theme Park
321 Whoopee Ave
Floor 7
Wichita, 67220

To who it may concern;

    I saw a advertisement in the Kansas City newspaper about jobs at wattathrill theme park in Wichita. I don't live there. I live in Emporia which is east of Wichita but I could live with my Grams all summer if I got the job. Please let me come for a audition. I could start as soon as you need me. Let me know when to come audition.

    I do a juggling act. I call it "Jugglin Johnny G" and I juggle in time with music that I play on my portable CD player that will get really loud. I'm very good at it because I started juggling when I was in elementery school where my dad was a gym teacher. He started me juggling to improve my coordination and I liked it so much I just kept doing it until I started getting jobs at birthday parties and church festivals and school fairs. I can juggle all kind of stuff—including, rubber balls, bowling pins and even dishes that make my parents really nervous. But that's not

Business Letter: Sample C (continued)

all. Also I do some mime work with my juggling routine for variety and giving my arms a rest. My friends says mimes are weirdos but I like it because you can walk right up to people and get in there face and make funny faces and things. Sometimes I like to scare little kids like that but usually they laff at me. Please call me soon. Thank you.

Jugglin Johnny

FOR THE TEACHER

SCORING

Business Letter: Sample C Evaluation

Holistic Scale

Rating: 2 points
Comments: This business letter shows that the writer does not understand the writing task. The writer's purpose is obscured by irrelevant information and vague language. The letter contains numerous formatting errors. Sentences are monotonous, and the writing shows a poor grasp of English-language conventions.

Analytical Scale: 7 Writing Traits

Ratings (High score is 5.)
Ideas and Content: 2   Sentence Fluency: 2
Organization: 1   Conventions: 2
Voice: 3   Presentation: 4
Word Choice: 2

Comments:
Ideas and Content: Information is limited and vague. The reader must make inferences to fill the gaps.

Organization: Ideas do not flow logically; this impairs the reader's understanding of the main idea. Formatting errors include an incomplete inside address, inappropriate salutation, incorrect paragraphing and indentation, and a poor closing.

Voice: Though generally appropriate for the audience, the language is neutral and flattened in tone.

Word Choice: The language is vague, communicating an imprecise message.

Sentence Fluency: Sentences are generally clear in meaning but lack structural variety. The writing lacks adequate transitions to help the reader make connections between ideas.

Conventions: The writer has a poor grasp of English-language conventions. Errors exist in punctuation, grammar, and spelling.

Presentation: The presentation is simple and clear.

Portfolio Assessment

FOR THE TEACHER
Portfolio Assessment in the Language Arts

Although establishing and using a portfolio assessment system requires a certain amount of time, effort, and understanding, an increasing number of teachers believe that the benefits of implementing such a system richly reward their efforts.

Language arts portfolios are collections of materials that display aspects of students' use of language. They are a means by which students can collect samples of their written work over time so that they and their teachers can ascertain how the students are developing as language users. Because reflection and self-assessment are built-in aspects of language arts portfolios, both also help students develop their critical-thinking and metacognitive abilities.

Each portfolio collection is typically kept in a folder, box, or other container to which items are added on a regular basis. The collection can include a great variety of materials, depending on the design of the portfolio assessment program, the kinds of projects completed inside and outside the classroom, and the interests of individual students. For example, portfolios may contain student stories, essays, sketches, poems, letters, journals, and other original writing, and they may also contain reactions to articles, stories, and other texts the student has read. Other materials that are suitable for inclusion in portfolios are drawings, photographs, audiotapes, and videotapes of students taking part in special activities; clippings and pictures from newspapers and magazines; and notes on favorite authors and on stories and books that the student hopes to read. Many portfolios also include several versions of the same piece of writing, demonstrating how the writing has developed through revision.

Finally, portfolios may contain logs of things the student has read or written, written reflections or assessments of portfolio work, and tables and explanations about the way the portfolio is organized. (A collection of forms that can be used to generate these items may be found at the end of this book.)

The Advantages of Portfolio Assessment

How can portfolio assessment help you meet your instructional goals? Here are some of the most important advantages of using portfolios:

- *Portfolios link instruction and assessment.* Traditional testing is usually one or more steps removed from the process or performance being assessed. However, because portfolio assessment focuses on performance—on students' actual use of language—portfolios are a highly accurate gauge of what students have learned in the classroom.
- *Portfolios involve students in assessing their own language use and abilities.* Portfolio assessment can provide some of the most effective learning opportunities available in your classroom. In fact, the assessment is

FOR THE TEACHER
Portfolio Assessment in the Language Arts (continued)

itself instructional: Students, as self-assessors, identify their own strengths and weaknesses. Furthermore, portfolios are a natural way to develop metacognition in your students. As the collected work is analyzed, the student begins to think critically about how he or she makes meaning while reading, writing, speaking, and listening. For example, the student begins to ask questions while reading, such as "Is this telling me what I need to know?" "Am I enjoying this author as much as I expected to?" "Why or why not?" While writing, the student may ask, "Am I thinking about the goals I set when I was analyzing my portfolio?" That's what good instruction is all about: getting students to use the skills you help them develop.

- *Portfolios invite attention to important aspects of language.* Because most portfolios include numerous writing samples, they naturally direct attention to diction, style, main idea or theme, author's purpose, and other aspects of language that are difficult to assess in other ways. The portfolio encourages awareness and appreciation of these aspects of language as they occur in literature and nonfiction as well as in the student's own work.

- *Portfolios emphasize language use as a process that integrates language behaviors.* Students who keep and analyze portfolios develop an understanding that reading, writing, speaking, and listening are all aspects of a larger process. They come to see that language behaviors are connected by thinking about and expressing one's own ideas and feelings.

- *Portfolios make students aware of audience and the need for a writing purpose.* Students develop audience awareness by regularly analyzing their portfolio writing samples. Evaluation forms prompt them to reflect on whether they have defined and appropriately addressed their audience. Moreover, because portfolios provide or support opportunities for students to work together, peers can often provide feedback about how well a student has addressed an audience in his or her work. Finally, students may be asked to consider particular audiences (parents, classmates, or community groups, for example) who will review their portfolios; they may prepare explanations of the contents for such audiences, and they may select specific papers to present as a special collection to such audiences.

- *Portfolios provide a vehicle for student interaction and cooperative learning.* Many projects that normally involve group learning produce material for portfolios. Portfolios, in turn, provide or support many opportunities for students to work together. Students can work as

> As they become attuned to audience, students automatically begin to be more focused on whether their work has fulfilled their purpose for writing. They begin to ask questions like, "Did I say what I meant to say? Could I have been clearer and more effective? Do I understand what this writer wants to tell me? Do I agree with it?" Speaking and listening activities can also be evaluated in terms of audience awareness and clarity of purpose.

Portfolio Assessment **121**

FOR THE TEACHER

Portfolio Assessment in the Language Arts *(continued)*

partners or as team members who critique each other's collections. For example, students might work together to prepare, show, and explain portfolios to particular audiences, such as parents, administrators, and other groups interested in educational progress and accountability.

- *Portfolios can incorporate many types of student expression on a variety of topics.* Students should be encouraged to include materials from different subject areas and from outside school, especially materials related to hobbies and other special interests. In this way, students come to see language arts skills as crucial tools for authentic, real-world work.

- *Portfolios provide genuine opportunities to learn about students and their progress as language users.* Portfolio contents can reveal to the teacher a great deal about the student's background and interests with respect to reading, writing, speaking, and listening. Portfolios can also demonstrate the student's development as a language user and reveal areas where he or she needs improvement.

FOR THE TEACHER
How to Develop and Use Portfolios

As you begin designing a portfolio program for your students, you may wish to read articles and reports that discuss the advantages of portfolio assessment.

Basic Design Features

For a portfolio program to be successful in the classroom, the program should reflect the teacher's particular instructional goals and the students' needs as learners. Teachers are encouraged to customize a portfolio program for their classrooms, although most successful portfolio programs share a core of essential portfolio management techniques. Following are suggestions that teachers will want to consider in customizing a portfolio program.

- *Integrate portfolio assessment into the regular classroom routine.* Teachers should make portfolio work a regular class activity by providing opportunities for students to work with their collections during class time. During these portfolio sessions, the teacher should promote analysis (assessment) that reflects his or her instructional objectives and goals.
- *Link the program to classroom activities.* Student portfolios should contain numerous examples of classroom activities and projects. To ensure that portfolios reflect the scope of students' work, some teachers require that certain papers and assignments be included.

You may want to require that certain papers, projects, and reports be included in the portfolio. Such requirements should be kept to a minimum so that students feel that they can include whatever they consider to be relevant to their language development.

- *Let students have the control.* Students can develop both self-assessment and metacognition skills when they select and arrange portfolio contents themselves. This practice also develops a strong sense of ownership: Students feel that their portfolios belong to them, not to the teacher. When students take ownership of their work, they accept more responsibility for their own language development. To encourage a sense of ownership on the part of students, portfolios should be stored where students can get at them easily, and students should have regular and frequent access to their portfolios.
- *Include students' creative efforts.* To ensure that the portfolios develop a range of language skills, encourage students to include samples of their creative writing, pieces they have written outside class, and publishing activities that they may have participated in, such as the production of a class magazine.

Portfolios that include such planning papers and intermediate drafts are called *working portfolios*. Working portfolios force the student to organize and analyze the material collected, an activity that makes clear to the student that language use is a process.

- *Make sure portfolios record students' writing process.* If portfolios are to teach language use as a process that integrates various language behaviors, they need to contain papers that show how writing grows out of planning and develops through revision. Portfolios should include notes, outlines, clippings, reactions to reading or oral presentations, pictures, and other materials that inspired the final product. Equally vital to the

Portfolio Assessment   **123**

FOR THE TEACHER

How to Develop and Use Portfolios (continued)

The act of selecting particular papers to show to special audiences—parents, another teacher, or the principal, to name a few—refines students' sense of audience. Preparing and presenting selected collections, called *show portfolios*, engages students in a more sophisticated analysis of their work and encourages them to visualize the audience for the show collection.

If students feel free to include writing and reading done outside class in their portfolios, you can discover interests, opinions, and concerns that can be touched on during conferences. In turn, by communicating interest in and respect for what engages the student, you can promote the success of the portfolio program.

portfolio collections are the different drafts of papers that demonstrate revision over a period of time. Such collections can promote fruitful, concrete discussions between student and teacher about how the student's process shaped the final product.

- *Rely on reactions to reading and listening.* If portfolios are to link and interrelate language behaviors, students must be encouraged to include reactions to things they read and hear. During conferences, teachers may want to point out how some of the student's work has grown out of listening or reading.
- *Encourage students to consider the audience.* Portfolio building prompts students to think about the audience because, as a kind of publication, the portfolio invites a variety of readers. Students will become interested in and sensitive to the reactions of their classmates and their teacher, as well as to the impact of the collections on any other audiences that may be allowed to view them.
- *Promote collaborative products.* Portfolios can promote student collaboration if the program sets aside class time for students to react to one another's work and to work in groups. This interaction can occur informally or in more structured student partnerships or team responses. In addition, many writing projects can be done by teams and small groups, and any common product can be reproduced for all participants' portfolios. Performance projects, speeches, and other oral presentations often require cooperative participation. Audiotapes and videotapes of group projects may be included in portfolios.
- *Let the portfolios reflect a variety of subject areas and interests.* The language arts portfolio should include material from subject areas other than language arts. Broadening the portfolio beyond the language arts classroom is important if the student is to understand that reading, writing, speaking, and listening are authentic activities—that is, that they are central to all real-world activities. Any extensive attempt to limit portfolio contents may suggest to students that these activities are important only in the language arts classroom.

Initial Design Considerations

Using what you have read so far, you can make some initial notes as guidelines for drafting your portfolio assessment design. You can complete a chart like the one on the next page to plan how you will use portfolios and what you can do to make them effective.

FOR THE TEACHER

How to Develop and Use Portfolios *(continued)*

▶ What are my primary goals in developing my students' ability to use language?	▶ How can portfolios contribute to meeting these goals?	▶ What design features can ensure this?

Portfolio Assessment

FOR THE TEACHER

How to Develop and Use Portfolios *(continued)*

Some key considerations for designing a portfolio program have been suggested. Other considerations will arise as you assess ways to use the portfolios. Here are some questions that will probably arise in the planning stages of portfolio assessment.

How can I introduce students to the concepts of portfolio management?

What examples of student work should go into the portfolios?

What should the criteria be for deciding what will be included?

How and where will the portfolio collections be kept?

Designing a Portfolio Program

How can I introduce students to the concepts of portfolio management?

One way to introduce students to portfolios is to experiment with a group of your students. If you use this limited approach, be sure to select students with varied writing abilities to get a sense of how portfolios work for students with a range of skill levels. To introduce portfolio assessment to them, you can talk to students either individually or as a group about what they will be doing. If other students begin expressing an interest in keeping portfolios, let them take part as well. The kind of excitement that builds around portfolio keeping almost guarantees that some students not included initially will want to get on board for the trial run; some may start keeping portfolios on their own.

You might let students help you design or at least plan some details of the system. After explaining both the reasons for keeping portfolios and the elements of the program that you have decided are essential, you can let students discuss how they think certain aspects should be handled. Even if you decide you want students to make important decisions concerning the program's design, you will need to have a clear idea of what your teaching objectives are and of what you will ask students to do.

What examples of student work should go into the portfolios?

Portfolios should reflect as much as possible the spectrum of your students' language use. What you want to ensure is that student self-assessment leads to the understanding that language skills are essential to all learning. For this to happen, portfolios should contain writing, speaking, and listening activities that relate to a number of subject areas and interests, not just to the language arts. Moreover, the portfolio should include final, completed works as well as drafts, notes, freewriting, and other samples that show the student's thinking and writing process.

FINAL PRODUCTS Students should consider including pieces that are created with a general audience in mind; writing that is communicative and intended for particular audiences; and writing that is very personal and that is used as a method of thinking through situations, evaluating experiences, or musing simply for enjoyment. The portfolios can contain a variety of finished products, including

- original stories, dialogue, and scripts
- poems

FOR THE TEACHER

How to Develop and Use Portfolios (continued)

- essays, themes, sketches
- song lyrics
- original videos
- video or audio recordings of performances
- narrative accounts of experiences
- correspondence with family members and friends
- stream-of-consciousness pieces
- journals of various types

Examples of various types of journals that students might enjoy keeping are described below.

Keeping Journals

A journal is an excellent addition to a portfolio—and one that teachers report is very successful. Journal keeping develops the habit of recording one's observations, feelings, and ideas. At the same time, journal writing is an excellent way to develop fluency. Specifically, it can help tentative writers to overcome the reluctance to put thoughts down as words. Journal keeping can be a bridge over inhibitions to writing and can become a student's favorite example of his or her language use. These benefits support the addition of journals to the portfolio.

Success with journals in encouraging young writers has led teachers to experiment with a variety of types:

PERSONAL JOURNAL This form of journal allows the writer to make frequent entries (regularly or somewhat irregularly) on any topic and for any purpose. This popular and satisfying kind of journal writing develops writing fluency and reveals to students the essential relationship between thinking and writing. (If the journal is kept in the portfolio, you may wish to remind students that you will be viewing it. Tell students to omit anything they would not be comfortable sharing.)

LITERARY JOURNAL OR READER'S LOG This journal provides a way of promoting open-ended and freewheeling responses to student reading. Students are usually allowed to structure and organize these journals in any way that satisfies them. As a collection of written responses, the literary journal is a valuable source of notes for oral and written expression; it can also give students ideas for further reading. Finally, the literary journal is another tool that reveals to students that reading, writing, and thinking are interrelated.

TOPICAL JOURNAL This style of journal is dedicated to a particular interest or topic. It is a valuable experience for students to be allowed to express themselves freely about a specific topic—a favorite hobby, pastime, or issue, for example.

Portfolio Assessment **127**

FOR THE TEACHER
How to Develop and Use Portfolios *(continued)*

As with the literary journal, the topical journal can point students toward project ideas and further reading.

DIALOGUE JOURNAL For this journal format, students select one person—a classmate, friend, family member, or teacher, for example—with whom to have a continuing dialogue. Dialogue journals help develop audience awareness and can promote cooperative learning. If students in your class are keeping dialogue journals with each other, be prepared to help them decide in whose portfolio the journal will go. (Because making copies may be too time consuming or expensive, you could help students arrange alternate custody, or have them experiment by keeping two distinct journals.)

Fragments and Works in Progress

Portfolios should include, in addition to finished products, papers showing how your students are processing ideas as readers, writers, speakers, and listeners. Drafts that show how writing ideas are developed through revision are especially helpful as students assess their work. Items that demonstrate how your language users are working with their collections can include

- articles, news briefs, sketches, or other sources collected and used as the basis for written or oral projects. These sources may include pictures created or collected by students and used for inspiration for the subject.
- reading-response notes that have figured in the planning of a paper and have been incorporated into the final work. Some notes may be intended for future projects.
- other notes, outlines, or evidence of planning for papers written or ready to be drafted
- pieces in which the student is thinking out a problem, considering a topic of interest or behavior, or planning something for the future. These pieces may include pro and con arguments, persuasive points, and reactions to reading.
- freewriting, done either at school or at home
- early versions (drafts) of the latest revision of a piece of writing
- notes analyzing the student's latest draft, which may direct subsequent revision
- solicited reactions from classmates or the teacher
- a published piece accompanied by revised manuscripts showing edits

FOR THE TEACHER

How to Develop and Use Portfolios *(continued)*

- correspondence from relatives and friends to which students have written a response or to which students need to respond
- journal or diary entries that are equivalent to preliminary notes or drafts of a piece of writing
- tapes of conversations or interviews to which a piece of writing refers or on which it is based

Discourage the inclusion of workbook sheets, unless they contain ideas for future student writing; they tend to obscure the message that language development is a process, a major component of which is the expression of student ideas and opinions.

While test results in general do not make good contents for portfolios, performance assessments can provide a focused example of both language processing and integration of reading and writing skills. Such performance tests are now frequently structured as realistic tasks that require reading, synthesizing, and reacting to particular texts. More often than not, these assessments guide the student through planning stages and a preliminary draft. (These parts of the assessment are rarely rated, but they lend themselves directly to self-analysis and should definitely be included with the final draft.)

What should the criteria be for deciding what will be included?

Teachers often want to ensure that students keep certain kinds of papers in the portfolios, while also affirming students' need for a genuine sense of ownership of their collections. Achieving a balance between these two general objectives may not be as difficult as it seems. Students can be informed at the time that they are introduced to the portfolio concept that they will be asked to keep certain items as one part of the overall project. Almost certainly, it will be necessary to explain at some point that the collections are to be working portfolios and that certain records—including many of the forms provided in this booklet—will also need to be included. As they become accustomed to analyzing the papers in their portfolios, students can be encouraged or required to select the contents of their portfolios, using criteria that they develop themselves. Teachers can help students articulate these criteria in informal and formal conferences. Following are criteria teachers or students might consider:

You might want to brainstorm a list of things that could be kept in your students' portfolios and then prioritize the items on your list according to which ones you think will be essential for students' development.

- papers that students think are well done and that therefore represent their best efforts, or papers that were difficult to complete
- subjects that students enjoyed writing about, or texts they have enjoyed reading; things that they think are interesting or will interest others
- things that relate to reading or writing that students intend to do in the future, including ideas that may be developed into persuasive essays, details to support positions on issues, and reactions to favorite literary texts

FOR THE TEACHER

How to Develop and Use Portfolios *(continued)*

- papers that contain ideas or procedures that students wish to remember
- incomplete essays or projects that presented some problem for the student. He or she may plan to ask a parent, teacher, or fellow student to react to the work or to earlier drafts.
- work that students would like particular viewers of the portfolio (the teacher, their parents, their classmates, and so on) to see, for some reason. This criterion is one that will dictate selections for a show portfolio; it may also determine some of the papers selected for the overall collection.

After building their collections for some time, students should be able to examine them and make lists of their selection criteria in their own words. Doing so should balance out any requirements the teacher has set for inclusion and should ensure students' sense of ownership.

A final note on selection criteria for student portfolios: While portfolios should certainly contain students' best efforts, too often teachers and students elect to collect only their "best stuff." An overemphasis on possible audiences that might view the collection can make it seem important that the collection be a show portfolio. Preparing show portfolios for particular audiences can require students to assess their work in order to decide what is worth including. That is a worthwhile experience, but once the preparation for the show has been completed, student self-assessment ends.

How and where will the portfolio collections be kept?

Part of the fun of keeping portfolios is deciding what the holders for the collections will look like. In a few classrooms, portfolio holders are standardized, but in most classes, the students are allowed to create their own. Many teachers allow students to furnish their own containers or folders, as long as these are big enough to hold the collections without students' having to fold or roll the papers—and not so large as to create storage problems. In addition, many teachers encourage their students to decorate their portfolio holders in unique, colorful, personal, and whimsical ways. Allowing this individuality creates enthusiasm for the project. It also helps students develop a genuine sense of ownership, an important attitude to foster if this system is to succeed.

The kinds of holders that students are likely to bring to school include household cardboard boxes, stationery boxes, folders of various types, paper or plastic shopping bags, computer paper boxes, and plastic and cardboard containers for storing clothing and other items. It would be a good idea to

> Start collecting some samples of holders you can show when you introduce portfolio management to your students. Decorate at least one sample, or have a young friend or relative do it. At the same time, be thinking about areas in your classroom where the collections can be kept.

PORTFOLIO ASSESSMENT

130 Holt Assessment: Writing, Listening, and Speaking

FOR THE TEACHER
How to Develop and Use Portfolios *(continued)*

have several different examples to show students when discussing how they will keep their papers. It is also a good idea to have some holders on hand for students who are unable to find anything at home that they think is suitable, and for use as replacements for unworkable holders some students may bring, such as shoe boxes that are too small to hold the portfolio items.

The resulting storage area will probably not be neatly uniform but will not necessarily be unattractive, either. Teachers who want a tidier storage area might find similar boxes to pass out to all students, who are then allowed to personalize them in different ways.

The amount of space available in a particular classroom will, of course, determine where students keep their collections, but it is vital that the area be accessible to students. It will save a great deal of inconvenience during the school year if the portfolios are on open shelves or on an accessible ledge of some kind and are not too far from students. If students can retrieve and put away their portfolios in less than a minute or two, there will be many instances when portfolio work can be allowed. Deciding where to keep the portfolios is a decision that may be put off until students know enough about the process to help make the decision.

Open access to portfolios does create the possibility of students looking at classmates' collections without permission and without warning. Remind students not to include in their portfolio anything they would not want others to see. A caution from the teacher could save a student from a wounding embarrassment.

FOR THE TEACHER
Conferencing with Students

If you are new at conducting portfolio conferences, ask a student who has kept one or more papers to sit down and talk with you. Talk with the student about what he or she thinks is strong about the paper, how it came to be written, and what kind of reading or research the student undertook. See how well you can promote an open-ended conversation related to the topic of the paper and to language use.

Think about what you could do to ensure a productive portfolio conference that would be helpful and worthwhile to students.

The regular informal exchanges between teacher and student about portfolio content are obviously very important, but the more formal conferences that anchor a successful program are of equal if not greater importance. Conferences are evidence that both the teacher and the student take the portfolio collection seriously and that the usefulness of the portfolio depends on an ongoing analysis of it. By blocking out time to conduct at least four formal conferences with each student each year, the teacher demonstrates a commitment to the program and a genuine interest in each student's progress.

Conducting Portfolio Conferences

The conference should proceed as a friendly but clearly directed conversation between the student and the teacher. The focus of the conference should be on how the use of language serves the student's needs and interests. This focus translates, in the course of the conference, into helping each student reflect on why and how he or she reads and writes.

Teachers will want to discuss with students the quantity of recent writing compared with that of previous time periods, the kinds of writing that the student has done, and the student's purposes for writing. Teachers will also want to discuss how the inclusions in the portfolio came to be and whether the pieces represent experiences and ideas the student has enjoyed and thinks are important. Teachers should let students know that the portfolio documents say something important about the individual student's life. In fact, a significant portion of the conference may be dedicated to learning about the student's interests. Here are a few examples of the types of statements that might elicit a helpful response:

- You seem to know a lot about deep-sea diving.
- Where did you learn all those details?
- Have you looked for books about deep-sea diving?
- What kinds of things could you write about deep-sea diving?

The student, too, should feel free to ask questions:

- Which pieces seem the best to the teacher and why?
- Is it always necessary to write for an audience?
- What if I *want* an idea or thought to remain private, though written?
- If I don't know how to spell a certain word, is it OK to just keep writing and look it up later?

FOR THE TEACHER
Conferencing with Students *(continued)*

These examples show how the conference can provide powerful, effective opportunities to teach and to guide language development. The conference conversations between the teacher and the student should be as unique as the individual student who joins the teacher in this exchange.

Ideally, each student will look forward to the conference as a time when student and teacher pay close attention to what the student has done; how the student feels about that performance; and what the student's needs and goals are. Such conferences encourage students to accept responsibility for their own development.

The following guidelines will help the teacher make the most of portfolio conferences.

Conference Guidelines

- *Conferences should be conducted without interruption.* Plan creatively: Perhaps a volunteer assistant can manage the rest of the class during meetings. Or, assign to other students learning activities or other work that does not disrupt your exchange with the student. It may be necessary to conduct the conference outside class time.

- *Keep the focus on the student.* Make the conference as much like an informal conversation as possible by asking questions that will emphasize the student's interests, attitudes toward writing, and favorite topics. Demonstrate that you care about what the student thinks and likes. You can also show that you respect the way a student's individuality is manifested in language use.

- *Let the conversation develop naturally.* Be an active listener: Give full attention to what the student is saying. The student's contribution is likely to suggest a question or comment from you, resulting in a genuine and natural exchange. There may be opportunities to get back to questions you had hoped to ask, but teachers should respect the course that the exchange takes and realize that some of their planned questions will need to be dropped. Good listening on the part of the teacher will help create successful conferences that address individual student interests and needs.

- *Be sincere but not judgmental.* Avoid evaluating or passing judgment on interests or aspects of the student's language use. On the other hand, try to avoid continually expressing approval and thereby creating a situation in which the student tries to respond in a way that will win favor: The conference will then lose its focus on the individual's language needs and development.

For many teachers, the time and planning that the conference demands constitute the most difficult aspect of portfolio assessment. Think about how you can use all the resources at your disposal, and don't forget to enlist students' help. Ask them to help you schedule meetings, and request their cooperation so that the system functions smoothly.

Questions will undoubtedly occur to you while reviewing the student's portfolio. It may be useful to have a few notes to remind you of things you would like to ask. Do not, however, approach a conference with a list that dictates the exchange with the student.

FOR THE TEACHER
Conferencing with Students (continued)

Don't hesitate to use the conference as a means of getting to know the student better by learning about his or her interests, pastimes, concerns, and opinions. This can be time well spent, particularly if it demonstrates to the student that the various aspects of his or her life can be very closely connected to the use and development of language arts skills.

Shortly after the conference, the student can translate his or her notes to a worksheet like the goal-setting form in this book, which will ask the student to elaborate on the objectives that have been established.

- *Keep the conversation open and positive.* It is fine to ask questions that direct the focus back to the collection, as long as that leads in turn to a discussion of ideas and content, the process of writing, and indications of the student's strengths and progress as a language user. In general, however, teachers should ask questions that promise to open up discussion, not shut it down. Phrase questions and comments so that they invite elaboration and explanation.
- *Gear the conference toward goal setting.* Identify and come to an agreement about the goals and objectives the student will be working on during the next time period.
- *Limit the attention devoted to usage errors.* If the student needs to focus on mechanical or grammatical problems, suggest that over the next time period the student pay particular attention to these problems when editing and revising. Do not, however, turn the session into a catalogue of language errors encountered. Keep in mind that if there are four conferences and each one tactfully encourages a focus on just one or two examples of nonstandard mechanical usage, it is possible to eliminate from four to eight high-priority errors during the course of a school year.
- *Keep joint notes with the student on the conference.* To keep a focus on the most important aspects of the conference, you and the student should keep notes. Frequently, student and teacher will record notes based on the same observation: For example, the student might write, "I like to use a lot of verbs at the beginning of my sentences, but maybe I use too many." And the teacher might write, "Let's watch to see how often Cody frontshifts sentence elements for emphasis." The student might write, "Look for a novel about the Civil War." The teacher might note, "Find a copy of *The Killer Angels* for Cody if possible." When the two participants make notes on the same sheet, side by side, the notes on the same point will roughly correspond. The teacher and the student can even write at the same time if they can position the note sheet in a way that will facilitate this.

Keep in mind that conference notes frequently serve as a reference point for an action plan that is then more fully considered on the goal-setting worksheet.

Types of Student-Teacher Conferences

In addition to the scheduled conference, there are several other types of conferences that teachers can conduct as a part of portfolio assessment:

FOR THE TEACHER
Conferencing with Students *(continued)*

GOAL CLARIFICATION CONFERENCES If a student appears to be having trouble using the portfolio system, a goal clarification conference can be scheduled. The meeting's focus should be to help the student clarify and articulate objectives so that work on the collection is directed and productive.

It is important that this session not be perceived as being overly critical of the student. Be supportive and positive about the collection; try to generate a discussion that will lead to clear goals for the student. These objectives can be articulated on a goal-setting worksheet, which the teacher can help the student fill out.

PUBLICATION STAFF CONFERENCES Students who are publishing pieces they write may frequently meet as teams or in staff conferences to select pieces from their portfolios. They may also discuss possible revisions of manuscripts they hope to publish. Teachers may enjoy observing and even participating in these but should let students direct them as much as possible.

Other class projects and collaborative activities can generate similar student conferences that may involve portfolio collections.

INFORMAL OR ROVING CONFERENCES In these conferences, teachers consult with students about their portfolios during impromptu sessions. For example, at any time a teacher might encounter a student with an important and intriguing question, or spot confusion or a situation developing into frustration for a self-assessor. Often the situation calls for effective questioning and then good listening, just as in the regularly scheduled conferences.

FOR THE TEACHER
Questions and Answers

The questions that follow are frequently asked by teachers who are thinking about instituting a portfolio management system.

- How can I make my students familiar and comfortable with the idea of creating portfolios?
- How often should my students work on their portfolios?
- How can I keep the portfolios from growing too bulky to manage and analyze effectively?
- Should I grade my students' portfolios?
- Who else, besides the student and me, should be allowed to see the portfolio?
- How can I protect against the possible negative effects of allowing a wide variety of persons to see students' portfolios?

How can I make my students comfortable with portfolios?

Teachers will, of course, want to begin by describing what portfolios are and what they are designed to accomplish. One way to help students visualize portfolios is to point out that some professionals keep portfolios:

- Artists usually keep portfolios to show prospective clients or employers what kind of work they can do. In a sense, an artist's studio is one big working portfolio, full of projects in various stages of completion.
- Photographers, architects, clothing designers, interior designers, and a host of other professionals keep portfolios full of samples of their work.
- Models carry portfolios of pictures showing them in a variety of styles and situations.
- Some writers keep portfolios of their work.
- People who invest their money in stocks and bonds call a collection of different investments a portfolio.

Teachers can encourage students' interest by inviting to the classroom someone who can exhibit and explain a professional portfolio. Teachers might also show students an actual language arts portfolio created by a student in another class or school. Some teachers put together a portfolio of their own and use it as an example for their students.

After this or another introduction, you might share the following information with students:

- Explain what kinds of things will go into the portfolios and why. Students can choose what to include in their collections, but teachers can indicate that a few items will be required, including some records. Without introducing all the records to be used, teachers might show and explain basic forms, such as logs. If forms filled out by students are available, use them as examples.

FOR THE TEACHER

Questions and Answers (continued)

- Stress that portfolios will be examined regularly. If the working portfolios will be available to parents or others, be sure to inform students. If you plan for others to see only show portfolios, this might be a good time to introduce this kind of portfolio.
- Show examples of holders that might be used, and explain where they will be kept. Students can be involved in making decisions about how and where portfolios will be housed.

How often should my students work on their portfolios?

The answer is "regularly and often." Teachers should schedule half-hour sessions weekly; ideally, there will be time almost every day when students can work on their collections. The Scheduling Plan on the next page shows activities that should occur regularly in your program.

How can I keep the portfolios from growing too bulky to manage and analyze effectively?

Because portfolios are intended to demonstrate students' products and processes over time, collections should be culled only when necessary. However, working portfolios can become simply too big, bulky, and clumsy to organize and analyze. If some students find their collections too unwieldy to work with, encourage them to try one of the following techniques:

- Cull older pieces except for those that stand as the best work examples. Put the removed contents into a separate holder and complete an *About This Portfolio* record. Explain on the record that the work consists of less-favored work, and have students take it home for parents to examine and/or save. Photocopies of later work that you consider more successful can be included as comparison.
- Close the whole collection, except for writing not yet completed, notes and records the student intends to use, and other idea files. Send the entire collection home with an explanation record, and start a new portfolio.
- Cull from the collection one or more show portfolios for particular audiences, such as parents, other relatives, other teachers, administrators, or supervisors. After the show portfolio has been viewed, return it to the rest of the collection. Start a new portfolio, beginning with the ideas in progress.

Some teachers have their students prepare a larger decorated box to take home at the beginning of the school year. This container eventually holds banded groups of papers culled during the year. Students then have one repository for their entire portfolio collection, which they can keep indefinitely.

Portfolio Assessment

FOR THE TEACHER

Questions and Answers (continued)

▶ **SCHEDULING PLAN FOR PORTFOLIO ASSESSMENT**

Activity	Frequency	The Student	The Teacher
Keeping logs	As writing and other language experiences are completed; daily if necessary	Makes the entries on the *Writing Record*	Encourages the student to make regular entries and discusses with the student indications of progress, developing interests, etc.
Collecting writing samples, reactions to reading, entries that reflect on oral language	As drafts and reactions to reading become available; can be as often as daily	Selects materials to be included	Can select materials to be included; may require some inclusions
Keeping journal(s)	Ongoing basis; daily to at least once a week	Makes regular entries in one or more journals	Analyzes journal writing discreetly and confidentially
Adding notes, pictures, clippings, and other idea sources	Weekly or more often	Clips and collects ideas and adds them to appropriate place in the portfolio	Reacts to student's idea sources (every month or so); discusses with student how he or she will use them
Explaining, analyzing, evaluating inclusions	Weekly; at least every other week	Uses forms for evaluating and organizing work to analyze and describe individual pieces included	Analyzes inclusions and student analysis of them at least four times a year—before conferences
Completing summary analyses	Monthly and always before conference	Completes a *Summary of Progress* record while comparing it with previously completed summary	Completes selected progress reports at least four times a year—before conferences, relying on student summaries and previously completed records
Conferencing—informal	Ongoing; ideally, at least once a week	Freely asks teacher for advice as often as needed; shares emerging observations with teacher	Makes an effort to observe student working on portfolio at least every two weeks and to discuss one or more specific new inclusions and analyses
Conferencing—formal	At least four times a year	Prepares for conference by completing summaries; discusses portfolio contents and analysis of them with teacher; devises new goals; takes joint notes	Prepares for conference with evaluative analyses; discusses portfolio contents and analysis with student; establishes new goals; takes joint notes
Preparing explanation of portfolio and analysis of it for a particular audience	As occasion for allowing other audiences access arises	Thoughtfully fills out the *About This Portfolio* form	Keeps student advised as to when other audiences might be looking at the student's collection and who the viewer(s) will be
Reacting to a fellow student's paper or portfolio	When it is requested by a "partner" or other classmate	Conferences with peer	Encourages collaboration whenever possible

PORTFOLIO ASSESSMENT

FOR THE TEACHER

Questions and Answers *(continued)*

Should I grade my students' portfolios?

Teachers might be tempted to grade portfolios to let students know that they are accountable for their work; teachers may also feel that a grade legitimizes—or at least recognizes—the time and effort that goes into successful portfolio assessment. Finally, many parents, school supervisors, and administrators will expect the teacher to grade the portfolio. These reasons notwithstanding, most portfolio experts recommend that portfolios not be graded. Keep in mind that the collection will contain papers that have been graded. A grade for the collection as a whole, however, risks undermining the goals of portfolio management. Grading portfolios may encourage students to include only their "best" work, and that practice may convey the message that student self-assessment is not taken seriously. Think about it: How would you feel if someone decided to incorporate your journal entries, your collection of ideas that interest you, and other notes and informal jottings into a package that was being rated and given a grade?

Who, besides the student and me, should see the portfolio?

This question raises some of the same concerns as the issue of grading portfolios. Teachers may feel some responsibility to let parents, a supervisor, the principal, and fellow faculty members know how the program is proceeding and what it shows about the progress of individuals or of the class as a whole. It is important to balance the benefits of showing portfolios to outside audiences against the possible adverse effects—the risk of inhibiting students, diminishing their sense of ownership, or invading their privacy. Above all, the primary aims of portfolio assessment must be kept in mind.

Following are some suggestions for showing portfolios, with respect to the audience involved.

PARENTS OR GUARDIANS Family members will almost certainly be viewing the portfolio in one form or another. If parents or other responsible adults are to view collections only on more formal occasions, such as back-to-school night or during unscheduled visits to the classroom, then students should be assisted in creating show portfolios. If, on the other hand, the teacher will show students' portfolios without the owners' knowledge or without offering them the opportunity to review the contents beforehand, the teacher must tell students this at the beginning of the year. Warning students of these unscheduled viewings may qualify their sense of ownership; it can also intensify their audience awareness.

Another way to involve parents in portfolio management is to let students plan a workshop on portfolio management geared for parents and others who are interested. Or, as suggested earlier, have students cull their collections periodically and take the materials home for their parents to see.

Portfolio Assessment **139**

FOR THE TEACHER

Questions and Answers *(continued)*

Again, if portfolios will be shown to other educators, students should be made aware of this before they start to build their collections.

SCHOOL SUPERVISORS AND PRINCIPALS Students' portfolios can demonstrate to fellow educators how youngsters develop as language users, thinkers, and people; they can also show the kind of learning that is taking place in the classroom. When working portfolios are shown, they are usually selected at random from those kept in the class, and the owner's identity is masked. Show portfolios are usually prepared specifically for this purpose. Whether teachers use working or show collections (assuming the state or school system does not mandate one) may depend partly on whether they think the audience will be able to appreciate that the working collections show process.

CLASSMATES Students may review their peers' portfolios as part of the program's assessment. Even if a particular program does not include a formal peer-review stage, remind students that peers may see their collections—either in the process of collaborative work or peer review, or because a student does not respect the privacy of others.

NEXT YEAR'S TEACHERS At the end of the school year, teachers can help students create a show portfolio for their next teacher or teachers. These portfolios should demonstrate the student's growth during the year and the potential of his or her best efforts. They should also indicate the most recent goals established by the teacher and the student, so that the new teacher knows how the student sees his or her language skills developing over the next year.

Encourage students to include finished projects as well as earlier drafts. Discuss what kinds of logs should be included, or have students prepare a brief report showing how goals have been met. A fresh table of contents would be useful, as would an explanation of what the show collection includes and what its purpose is. Teachers may want to let students make copies of some papers that they would also like to take home.

THE STUDENTS THEMSELVES At the end of the school year, portfolio contents can be sent home for parents to see and save, if they wish. Before doing this, teachers may wish to have students prepare a starter portfolio of ideas, writing, plans for reading, and so on, for next year.

How can I protect against the possible negative effects of allowing a wide variety of persons to see students' portfolios?

Whatever special reporting the teacher does with portfolios, he or she needs to offset any possible adverse effects by keeping the primary aims for portfolio assessment in mind.

FOR THE TEACHER

Questions and Answers *(continued)*

- The overall goal of the program is to develop students as language users. That goal should become the focus of joint student/teacher evaluation of the student's progress.
- Because another important goal is for students to develop a habit of self-assessment, the collections must be readily available to students.
- The emphasis should be on examining the process by looking at the product and the way it is produced. Each portfolio should be a working collection containing notes, drafts, and records of the evaluation of its contents.
- The activities assessed should integrate reading, writing, speaking, and listening.
- The portfolio should be controlled and owned by the student.
- The collections should include reactions to and applications of a variety of text and writing types—with a variety of purposes involving different audiences.

NAME _____ CLASS _____ DATE _____

Portfolio Table of Contents

Decide on the major categories for work in your portfolio. Then, in the sections below, list the categories you have chosen. The works themselves may be papers, speech notecards, videotapes, multimedia products, or any work you and your teacher agree should be included. In choosing categories, consider organizing work by topic, by genre (essays, poems, stories, and so on), by chronology (work completed by month, for example), by level of difficulty (work that was less difficult, somewhat difficult, and more difficult), or according to another plan.

Grade: _____ School year: _____

▶ WORK IN EACH SECTION	▶ WHY I PUT THIS WORK IN THIS SECTION
Section 1:	
title:	
title:	
title:	
title:	
Section 2:	
title:	
title:	
title:	
title:	
Section 3:	
title:	
title:	
title:	
title:	

PORTFOLIO ASSESSMENT

NAME _____ CLASS _____ DATE _____

SELF-EVALUATION

About This Portfolio

Use this form whenever you are preparing your portfolio for review by your teacher or another reader.

Grade: _____ School year: _____ When I began this portfolio: _____

▶ **How it is organized:**

▶ **What I think it shows about my progress . . .**

as a reader:

as a writer:

as a listener:

as a speaker:

GO ON ➡

PORTFOLIO ASSESSMENT

Portfolio Assessment **143**

NAME _____ CLASS _____ DATE _____

SELF-EVALUATION

About This Portfolio *(continued)*

▶ **Examples of My Best Work**

The best things I have read are—	Why I like them—
The best things I have written are—	Why I like them—
Other things in my portfolio that I hope you notice are— 1. 2. 3.	What they show—

144 Holt Assessment: Writing, Listening, and Speaking

NAME _____ CLASS _____ DATE _____

TO PARENT OR GUARDIAN

Home Review: What the Portfolio Shows

In the left-hand column of the chart below, I have noted what I believe this portfolio shows about your child's development in areas such as reading, writing, speaking, and listening. The right-hand column notes where you can look for evidence of that development.

A prime objective in keeping portfolios is to develop in students a habit of analyzing and evaluating their work. This portfolio includes work that the student has collected over a period of time. The student has decided what to include but has been encouraged to include different types of writing, responses to reading, and evidence of other uses of language. Many of the writings included are accompanied by earlier drafts and plans that show how the work has evolved from a raw idea to a finished piece of writing. The inclusion of drafts is intended to reinforce to the student that using language entails a process of revision and refinement.

▶ I believe that this portfolio shows—	▶ To see evidence of this, please notice—

Teacher's signature _____

Portfolio Assessment **145**

STUDENT'S NAME _____ CLASS _____ DATE _____

TO PARENT OR GUARDIAN

Home Response to the Portfolio

> Please answer any questions that seem important to you. Use the reverse side for any additional comments or questions.
> Parent or Guardian _____ Date _____

What did you learn from the portfolio about your child's reading?
_____
_____
_____

What did you learn from the portfolio about your child's writing?
_____
_____
_____

Were you surprised by anything in the portfolio? Why?
_____
_____

What do you think is the best thing in the portfolio? What do you like about it?
_____
_____

Do you have questions about anything in the portfolio? What would you like to know more about?
_____
_____
_____

What does the portfolio tell you about your child's progress as a writer, reader, and thinker?
_____
_____
_____

Do you think keeping a portfolio has had an effect on your child as a reader or writer—or in another way? If so, what?
_____
_____
_____
_____

Is there anything missing from the portfolio that you would have liked or had expected to see? If so, what?
_____
_____

PORTFOLIO ASSESSMENT

146 Holt Assessment: Writing, Listening, and Speaking

STUDENT'S NAME _____ CLASS _____ DATE _____

SELF-EVALUATION

Writing Record

▶ **Ratings:** ✓✓✓✓ One of my best! ✓✓ OK, but not my best
　　　　　　✓✓✓ Better if I revise it ✓ I don't like this one.

▶ Month/Day	▶ Title and type of writing	▶ Notes about this piece of writing	▶ Rating

Portfolio Assessment

NAME _____ CLASS _____ SCHOOL YEAR _____

SELF-EVALUATION

Spelling Log

▶ Word	▶ My misspelling	▶ How to remember correct spelling

NAME _____ CLASS _____ SCHOOL YEAR _____

Goal-Setting for Writing, Listening, and Speaking

▶ GOAL	▶ STEPS TO REACH GOAL	▶ REVIEW OF PROGRESS
Writing Goals		

GO ON

Portfolio Assessment **149**

NAME _____ CLASS _____ SCHOOL YEAR _____

Goal-Setting for Writing, Listening, and Speaking *(continued)*

▶ GOAL	▶ STEPS TO REACH GOAL	▶ REVIEW OF PROGRESS
Listening Goals		
Speaking Goals		

NAME _____ CLASS _____

SELF-EVALUATION

Summary of Progress: Writing, Listening, and Speaking

Complete this form before sitting down with your teacher or a classmate to assess your overall progress, set goals, or discuss specific pieces of your work.

Grade: _____ School year: _____ Date of summary: _____

▶ **What work have I done so far this year?**

Writing:

Listening:

Speaking:

▶ **What project do I plan to work on next?**

Writing:

Listening:

Speaking:

▶ **What do I think of my progress?**

What about my work has improved?

What needs to be better?

▶ **Which examples of work are my favorites and why?**

GO ON ▶

Portfolio Assessment   **151**

NAME _____ CLASS _____

SELF-EVALUATION

Summary of Progress: Writing, Listening, and Speaking *(continued)*

▶ **Which pieces of work need more revision, and what is needed?**

▶ **How has listening or speaking helped me in preparing for papers or other projects this year?**

▶ **What a classmate or the teacher thinks about my progress**

In writing—

In listening—

In speaking—

NAME _____ CLASS _____ DATE _____

SELF-EVALUATION

Writing Self-Inventory

▶ Questions and answers about my writing	▶ More about my answers
How often do I write?	What types of writing do I do?
Where, besides school, do I write?	What kind of writing do I do there?
Do I like to write?	Why or why not?
Of the things I have written, I like these best:	Why do I like them best?
What topics do I like to write about?	Why do I like to write about these topics?
Is anything about writing difficult for me? What?	Why do I think it is difficult?
Does reading help me to be a better writer or vice versa?	Why do I think this?
How important is learning to write well?	Why do I think this?

Portfolio Assessment **153**

NAME _____ CLASS _____ DATE _____

SELF-EVALUATION

Writing Process Self-Evaluation

Choose one paper from your portfolio, preferably one for which you have your prewriting notes and all your drafts. Use the chart below to analyze your writing process. Circle the numbers that most clearly indicate how well you meet the stated criteria in your writing process. The lowest possible total score is 5, the highest, 20.

1 = Do not meet these criteria
2 = Attempt to meet these criteria but need to improve
3 = Are fairly successful in meeting criteria
4 = Clearly meet these criteria

Title of paper _____

STAGE IN WRITING PROCESS	CRITERIA FOR EVALUATION	RATING
Prewriting	• Use prewriting techniques to find and limit subject and to gather details about subject • Organize details in a reasonable way	1 2 3 4
Writing	• Get most of ideas down on paper in a rough draft	1 2 3 4
Revising	• Do complete peer- or self-evaluation • Find ways to improve content, organization, and style of rough draft • Revise by adding, cutting, replacing, and moving material	1 2 3 4
Proofreading	• Correct errors in spelling, grammar, usage, punctuation, capitalization, and manuscript form	1 2 3 4
Publishing and Reflecting	• Produce a clean final copy in proper form • Share the piece of writing with others • Reflect on the writing process and on the paper's strengths and weaknesses	1 2 3 4

Additional Comments:

PORTFOLIO ASSESSMENT

154 Holt Assessment: Writing, Listening, and Speaking

NAME _____ CLASS _____ DATE _____

SELF-EVALUATION

Proofreading Strategies

Proofread your paper using one of the following steps. Put a check by the step you used.

_____   **1.** Read the paper backward word by word.

_____   **2.** Make a large card with a one- or two-inch-sized strip cut into it and read every word in the paper, one at a time, through the hole.

_____   **3.** Read the first sentence in your paper carefully. Put your left index finger on the punctuation mark that signals the end of that sentence. Now, put your right index finger on the punctuation mark that ends the second sentence. Carefully read the material between your fingers; then, move your left index finger to the end of the second sentence and your right to the end of the third sentence, and read carefully. Keep moving your fingers until you have carefully examined each sentence in the paper.

List the mistakes you discovered when proofreading.

_____

_____

_____

_____

_____

_____

_____

_____

_____

_____

_____

_____

Portfolio Assessment **155**

NAME _____ CLASS _____ DATE _____

PEER- AND SELF-EVALUATION

Proofreading Checklist

Read through the paper and then mark the following statements either **T** for true or **F** for false. If you are reviewing a classmate's paper, return the paper and checklist to the writer. After the writer has done his or her best to correct the paper, offer to assist if your help is needed.

Writer's name _____ Title of paper _____

_____ 1. The paper is neat.

_____ 2. Each sentence begins with a capital letter.

_____ 3. Each sentence ends with a period, question mark, or exclamation mark.

_____ 4. Each sentence is complete. Each has a subject and a predicate and expresses a complete thought.

_____ 5. Run-on sentences are avoided.

_____ 6. A singular verb is used with each singular subject and a plural verb with each plural subject.

_____ 7. Nominative case pronouns such as *I* and *we* are used for subjects; objective case pronouns such as *me* and *us* are used for objects.

_____ 8. Singular pronouns are used to refer to singular nouns, and plural pronouns are used to refer to plural nouns.

_____ 9. Indefinite pronoun references are avoided.

_____ 10. Each word is spelled correctly.

_____ 11. Frequently confused words, such as *lie/lay, sit/set, rise/raise, all ready/already,* and *fewer/less,* are used correctly.

_____ 12. Double negatives are avoided.

_____ 13. All proper nouns and proper adjectives are capitalized.

_____ 14. Word endings such as *–s, –ing,* and *–ed* are included where they should be.

_____ 15. No words have been accidentally left out or accidentally written twice.

_____ 16. Each paragraph is indented.

_____ 17. Apostrophes are used correctly with contractions and possessive nouns.

_____ 18. Commas or pairs of commas are used correctly.

_____ 19. Dialogue is punctuated and capitalized correctly.

_____ 20. Any correction that could not be rewritten or retyped is crossed out with a single line.

NAME _____ CLASS _____ DATE _____

PEER- AND SELF-EVALUATION

Record of Proofreading Corrections

Keeping a record of the kinds of mistakes you make can be helpful. For the next few writing assignments, list the errors you, your teacher, or your peers find in your work. If you faithfully use this kind of record, you'll find it easier to avoid troublesome errors.

Writer's name _____ Title of paper _____

Write sentences that contain errors in grammar or usage here.

Write corrections here.

Write sentences that contain errors in mechanics here.

Write corrections here.

Write misspelled words and corrections here.

Portfolio Assessment

NAME _____ CLASS _____ DATE _____

SELF-EVALUATION

Multiple-Assignment Proofreading Record

▶ **DIRECTIONS:** When your teacher returns a corrected writing assignment, write the title or topic on the appropriate vertical line at right. Under the title or topic, record the number of errors you made in each area. Use this sheet when you proofread your next assignment, taking care to check those areas in which you make frequent mistakes.

▶ **TITLE OR TOPIC OF ASSIGNMENT**

▶ **Type of Error**

- Sentence Fragments
- Run-on Sentences
- Subject-Verb Agreement
- Pronoun Agreement
- Incorrect Pronoun Form
- Use of Double Negative
- Comparison of Adjectives and Adverbs
- Confusing Verbs
- Irregular Verbs
- Noun Plurals and Possessives
- Capitalization
- Spelling
- End Punctuation
- Apostrophes
- Confusing Words
- Quotation Marks and Italics
- Comma or Paired Commas

PORTFOLIO ASSESSMENT

158 Holt Assessment: Writing, Listening, and Speaking

NAME _____ CLASS _____ DATE _____

SELF-EVALUATION

Listening Self-Inventory

▶ Questions and answers about my listening	▶ More about my answers
What kinds of music do I like to listen to?	Why do I like them?
What TV shows and movies are my favorites?	What do I like about them?
How well do I listen in school?	How much do I learn by listening?
Do I listen carefully to what my friends say?	What do I learn from them?
When is it difficult for me to listen?	What makes it difficult?
How do I use the praise and suggestions of others to improve my skills?	How do I feel about getting praise or suggestions for improvement?

Portfolio Assessment

NAME _____ CLASS _____ DATE _____

SELF-EVALUATION

Speaking Self-Inventory

▶ Questions and answers about my speaking	▶ More about my answers
How do I feel about speaking to friends?	What do I like to discuss with them?
How do I feel about talking to adults?	Why do I feel this way?
How do I feel about reciting or speaking to the class?	Why do I feel this way?
What is the most difficult thing about speaking?	Why is it difficult?
What techniques have I learned to improve my speaking?	How do I use these techniques with friends or in class?

PORTFOLIO ASSESSMENT

160 Holt Assessment: Writing, Listening, and Speaking

Skills Profile

Student's Name _____ Grade _____

Teacher's Name _____ Date _____

For each skill, write the date the observation is made and any comments that explain the student's development toward skills mastery.

▶ SKILL	▶ NOT OBSERVED	▶ EMERGING	▶ PROFICIENT
▶ **Writing**			
Writing Modes			
Write an editorial.			
Write a short story.			
Write a reflective essay.			
Write a historical research report.			
Write a descriptive essay.			
Write an essay analyzing a short story.			

Skills Profile *(continued)*

SKILL	NOT OBSERVED	EMERGING	PROFICIENT
Write a biographical narrative.			
Write an essay analyzing a novel.			
Write an autobiographical narrative.			
Write an essay analyzing nonfiction.			
Writing Process			
Prewriting			
• Choose a topic.			
• Identify purpose and audience.			
• Generate ideas and gather information about the topic.			

Skills Profile (continued)

SKILL	NOT OBSERVED	EMERGING	PROFICIENT
• Begin to organize the information.			
• Draft a thesis statement, or a sentence that expresses the main point.			

Writing a Draft

• State the main points and include relevant support and elaboration.			
• Follow a plan of organization.			

Revising

• Revise for content and style.			

Publishing

• Proofread for grammar, usage, and mechanics.			

Skills Profile (continued)

SKILL	NOT OBSERVED	EMERGING	PROFICIENT
• Publish the work, or share the finished writing with readers.			
• Reflect on the writing experience.			
Listening and Speaking			
Deliver and evaluate a persuasive speech.			
Deliver an oral presentation of a reflective essay.			
Deliver an oral research report.			
Present an oral response to a literary work.			
Deliver a multimedia presentation.			

Skills Profile *(continued)*

SKILL	NOT OBSERVED	EMERGING	PROFICIENT
Analyze strategies used by different forms of media.			
Perform an oral recitation of literature.			
Plan and organize the speech or presentation.			
Rehearse and deliver the presentation.			
Use effective verbal and nonverbal techniques.			
Use effective rhetorical techniques.			
Understand and identify logical fallacies and propaganda techniques.			